THE SCENT OF RAIN

Essence of Hope

Hope for a New Beginning when Life feels at an End.

Discover how to regain your purpose, reclaim your passion, and renew your life.

By

E. David Simons

DEDICATION

I dedicate this book to my Dad and Mom: Ken and Deanna Simons, my wife, Marianne, and our three children, Joshua David, Hannah Joy, and Sarah Grace.

CONTENTS

INTRODUCTION

The Scent of Rain—Essence of Hope

I see people not as problems to be solved but plants to be nourished. As such, may *The Scent of Rain—Essence of Hope* provide the necessary nutrients to cause your heart to beat again, your hope to rise above the ashes, your faith to shine in the darkest of nights and your voice to be truly heard for what it is; a sacred melody of His grace. If your life has been cut like a tree, leaving your dreams dead or dormant, your hopes crushed, your love lost, your passion stale, purpose aimless, and presence a mere ghost of whom you used to be, then my hope for all my readers is that soon, very soon, you too will get a whiff of the scent of rain from off these pages. The essence of hope, the understanding that soon new life can and will begin to sprout from that particular area of your heart, that looked, to you—and maybe to others—lifeless.

The Scent of Rain—Essence of Hope is a strategic, scriptural, scientific, and systematic approach of discovering and developing the ability to "bud" again in one's purpose, passion, and life.

Allow *The Scent of Rain—Essence of Hope* to be one of your life's manuals, aiding you in enhancing your experience of hope so your purpose, passion, and life will bud again in every season of life.

When Does One Need the Scent of Rain—Essence of Hope?

- When your purpose, passion, and life have wilted, weakened, and are worn out
- When you seem broken beyond repair

- When you seem too far gone
- When you seem nothing but damaged goods
- When you seem wounded
- When your soul can't sustain you
- When shame has left a searing stain
- When your dreams and hopes you wish to regain
- When the force of favor you wish to obtain
- When your cuts and scars remind you of pain
- When you have felt crushed to the ocean floor

God is a God of renewal. The goodness of God will come down like dew upon you. Everything God touches is changed. Extraordinary reversals of God. Death to life, emptiness to liberty. He is himself reversal, loss turned to restoration, and decay to renewal at His touch.

At the scent of rain - you will bud again. (Job 14:7-9)

The spirit and source from which I write to you today are reflected in this story:

This guy's walking down the street when he falls in a hole. The walls are so steep he can't get out.

A doctor passes by, and the guy shouts up, "Hey, you. Can you help me out?" The doctor writes a prescription, throws it down in the hole, and moves on.

Then a priest comes along, and the guy shouts, "Father, I'm down in this hole, can you help me out?" The priest writes out a prayer, throws it down in the hole, and moves on.

Then a friend walks by, "Hey, Joe, it's me, can you help me out?" And the friend jumps in the hole.

Our guy says, "Are you stupid? Now we're both down here."

The friend says, "Yeah, but I've been down here before, and I know the way out."

(Adapted from a story told on the "Noel" episode of "The West Wing," December 20, 2000, first airing.)

My friend, I am "Joe" to you. This book has been written out of the personal experience. My "tree" of purpose, passion, and life were ever so deeply cut;

however, through the practice of strategic skills and steps unpacked in this book, I experienced the scent of rain and purpose, passion, and life budded again!

Although different from what I had thought, it is better than I had imagined!

To everything, there is a season and a time for every purpose under the heaven. *The Scent of Rain—Essence of Hope* will assist you in "redeeming the time" and making the most of and transforming "lost" time into "found" time, with serendipitous fortune developing the skill set to navigate the cycles of life and transition successfully!

There is yet hope for a tree; there is hope for you and me! At the scent of rain, my purpose, passion, and life will bud again.

CHAPTER 1

First Fragrance of the Scent of Rain

T hroughout the past three decades, I've experienced God. Thirty years ago, amidst a season of drought, void of purpose, passion, and meaning of life, a summer shower of "heaven's rain" poured heavily through my soul, penetrating deep within my spirit, bringing immediately new buds of passion, purpose, and life. That summer July morning in 1981 at Whited Bible Camp within the old Tabernacle, comprised of cement floors and wooden pews, following Danny Thomas' message, the scent of rain flooded my heart, leaving its fragrance so fresh and unforgettable. In opening the blue-covered Bible to discover words of comfort, direction, or instruction, the pages fell open on Luke 4:18: "The Spirit of the Lord is upon Me, because He hath anointed me to preach the gospel unto the poor; he hath sent me to heal the brokenhearted, to preach deliverance to the captives, and recovering of sight to the blind to set at liberty them that are bruised." The scent of heaven's rain washed all my fears away, filling the void of purpose with buds of new life yet to be fully formed. I was called to be a messenger of good news, a purveyor of hope to the hurting, freedom to the bound, clarity to the confused, and light to those dim of vision. Thus a journey of 30 years began, which has traveled through five continents, 16 countries, and **each of the four life seasons: The High Points of Mountain Peaks, The Desert Doldrums, Wilderness Valleys, and Plains of Planning.** The following pages are not merely a prescription passed on to you by a physician, nor a prayer proposed unto you by a minister, but a life map from a fellow traveller who has been where you are and has discovered that through *The Scent of Rain—Essence* *of Hope,* one can reclaim purpose, passion, and life again. Yes, you have experienced some cuts, wounds, and scars; yet there is HOPE. You will bud and live again!

You are a TREE of possibility!

Regardless of when you've been wounded and cut, whether as a child, youth, young adult, spouse, parent or grandparent;

Regardless of how you've been wounded and cut: relationally, emotionally, mentally, physically, vocationally, financially, even ministerially;

Regardless of why you've been cut or who cut you, THERE IS HOPE. Hope beyond the scope of human limitations—hope that is found in *The Scent of Rain.*

"Mended" by Matthew West in "Live Forever"

When you see broken beyond repair
I see healing beyond belief
When you see too far gone
I see one step away from home

How many times can one heartbreak?
It was never supposed to be this way
Look in the mirror, but you find someone you never thought you'd be

Oh, but I can still recognize
The one I love in your tear-stained eyes
I know you might not see him now, so lift your eyes to me

When you see broken beyond repair
I see healing beyond belief
When you see too far gone
I see one step away from home

When you see nothing but damaged goods
I see something good in the making
I'm not finished yet
When you see wounded, I see mended

You see your worst mistake
But I see the price I paid
And there's nothing you could ever do, to lose what grace has won

So hold on, it's not the end
No, this is where love's work begins
I'm making all things new
And I will make a miracle of you

When you see broken beyond repair
I see healing beyond belief
When you see too far gone
I see one step away from home

When you see nothing but damaged goods
I see something good in the making
I'm not finished yet
When you see wounded, I see mended

I see my child, my beloved
The new creation you're becoming
You see the scars from when you fell
But I see the stories they will tell

You see worthless; I see priceless
You see pain, but I see a purpose
You see unworthy, undeserving
But I see you through eyes of mercy

CHAPTER 2

A Summer's Purse

"In the Journal of the American Medical Association, Jane McAdams told the story of her sixty-nine-year-old mother who had lived a life deeply marked by the Great Depression of the 1930s. The evidence showed in her frugality and utterly practical perspective on all material things. The only extravagance she had ever permitted herself, McAdams wrote, was a frilly nightgown kept in a bottom drawer, "In case I should ever have to go to the hospital."

That day had come. All the symptoms that made her visit the hospital necessary spoke of serious cancer, and McAdams feared the moment when she would have to tell her mother that the prognosis for the future was very poor. The daughter wondered, "Should I tell my mother? Does she already know? If not, does she suspect? Can I give her any hope? Is there any hope?"

As she wrestled with these questions, McAdams noted that her mother's birthday was approaching. Perhaps she could brighten her mother's day by purchasing a new nightgown because the one that had been in the bottom drawer was yellowed, limp, and unattractive. So she purchased and presented a new nightgown and matching robe, thinking,

"If I could not hope to cure her disease, at least I could make her feel like the prettiest patient in the entire hospital."

McAdams described how her mother studied the gown after the package was opened. And after a while, she pointed to the wrapping and the gown and said to her daughter, "Would you mind returning it to the store? I don't really want it." Then pick up the paper, she pointed to a display advertisement and said, "This is what I want if you could get that." What she pointed to was a display advertisement for expensive designer summer purses.

McAdams' reaction was one of disbelief. Why would her mother, so careful about extravagances, want an expensive summer purse in January, one that she could not possibly use until June? She would not live until spring, let alone summer.

Almost immediately, McAdams was ashamed and appalled at her clumsiness, ignorance, insensitivity, call it what you will. With a shock, she realized her mother was finally asking her what she thought about the illness, asking if she thought her mother was going to live even six months. And her mother was telling McAdams that if she showed a belief that her mother would live until then, then she would do it. She would not let that expensive purse go unused.

That day, McAdams returned the gown and robe and bought the summer purse.

That was many years ago. The purse is worn out and long gone, as are at least half a dozen others. And next week McAdams' mother flies to California to celebrate her 83rd birthday. Her daughter's gift to her? The most expensive designer purse she could find. She'll use it well." 1

T he gift of restorative grace to a broken world person is the gift not of a nightgown that announces death but of a summer purse that says there is life after failure. That is the message of the Cross and the empty tomb. And it must be the message of the church to the broken world person. To all who have been cut like a tree. This is our mandate—this must be our mission—to be as the scent of rain: purveyors of hope,

Hannah, my oldest daughter's Summer Purse letter to her Nana-my Mom while she was battling breast cancer. Hannah was 13yrs old.

> *"Dear Nana and Papa:*
>
> *First of I just wanted to tell you both that I dearly miss you and love you. I can't wait to spend two weeks in Maine with you next summer, and I know it's going to be so fun. Lately, I have been thinking about how you two have loved me even when I was six years old and when I heard your names, I thought presents! Thankfully that stage passed at eight years old. I thank God that both of you are living in the time that I remember everything. I love the little memories that you both gave me. For example, Grandma, you and I made my small quilt with the designs on it. I love all the memories, and it's like taking a bit of a great chocolate cupcake. I can't wait to make some more, love you so much.*
>
> *Loving Granddaughter Hannah"*

By the grace of God: my mother survived breast cancer and was able to spend the next summer and each following summer with Hannah and Sarah, building memories together.

Key Question: Who Within Your Sphere of Influence Needs Not a "Nightgown" of Death but a "Summer's Purse" of Life and Hope, of The Scent of Rain?

Perhaps you are lying within circumstances and situations that speak death, that smell of death, and are seen as failures: Today, I give you your "summer's purse." There is yet hope—there is always HOPE—and your best and brightest days are yet to be! Today, as an experienced rain scent smeller, I'm here to announce to you that rain is on the way! Hold on, have hope, and receive this book as your "summers' purse"—for hope is alive and your purpose, passion, and life will bud again!

Time began and will end in a garden, where God's presence is as the "dew" in the morning. Let's go back in time to discover where we first read of the scent of rain.

Job: Oldest Historical Biblical Character to Experience the Scent of Rain and the Essence of Hope

For there is hope for a tree if it is cut down, that it will sprout again, and that its tender shoots will not cease. Though its root may grow old in the earth, and its stump may die in the ground: YET through the SCENT of Water (RAIN), it will bud and bring forth branches like a plant. (Job 14:7-9, NKJ version)

The scent of rain gave hope for one man to find purpose, passion, and life again—a man named Job. Considered to be one of the oldest characters mentioned in the Bible, Job perhaps serendipitously discovered the strikingly similar parallel between his personal life and the patterns of nature, as revealed in the signature scriptural passage of the Book of Job.

By the time you reach Job 14:7-9, you will meet a man who has suffered the excruciating pain of being cut in every which way imaginable. He, who was once on the summit of a mountain-top experience, having reached the success of epic proportions as seen in being a large landowner, owning thousands of livestock, dozens of employees, feasting on the best food available, providing employment for all of his 10+ children and spouses, has now in Chapter 14 found himself alone, abandoned emotionally by his wife, absent of all his children who were killed instantly in a tornado, whose only affections were found in the licks of a man's best friend—his dogs, as they licked his wounds. Job had lost it all: purpose, passion, the fulfillment of life. He lay amidst an earth-crusted floor, scraping his wounds with broken shards of clay.

His cuts were many, open and seeping of fluids: economically, relationally, emotionally, vocationally cut, his identity was cut, his masculinity was cut, it seemed that even his destiny was cut—leaving little if any, hope for life itself. Life, as Job knew it, had ended.

Ever have a bad day? Remember Job. Yes—remember Job, although remembering alone may not return the voice of your child unto you, the warmth of a spouse's embrace, the security of your familiar workplace, the confidence of a checking account above zero, the sense of meaning amidst all the madness, the comfort of courage within the chaos. Yet remembering Job might lead you to discover and develop the skills and steps of enhancing the scent of rain to reclaim your purpose, passion, and life again. It has for me, and I hope that you will indeed smell the scent of rain to bud again.

Possibly the oldest book in the Bible, Job reads like the most modern. Its extreme portrayal—one man confronting the abyss in a world that makes no sense—foreshadows the predicament of modern humanity. People who reject nearly everything else in the Bible keep coming back to Job for inspiration. Its recurring theme—how can a good God allow suffering? Is the only problem worth discussing? The problem of pain is a modern obsession, and the ancient man Job expressed it as well as it has ever been expressed. Job is the Bible's prime case study of disappointment with God, and as such, it seems to anticipate whatever disappointment any of us may feel.

Job reveals the very worst things happening to the very best person. Although all but a few pages of Job deal with the problem of pain, I am concluding that Job is not really about the problem of pain. Although suffering is seen vividly throughout the book of Job, it is not the main theme.

Seen as a whole, Job is primarily about faith in its starkest form. The most crucial battle, as shown in Job, takes place inside us. Will we trust and hope in God? Job teaches us that at the moment when faith is hardest and least likely, then faith is most necessary and needed. His struggle presents a glimpse of what the Bible elsewhere spells out—the remarkable truth that our choices matter, not just to us, and our destiny, but amazingly, to God Himself and the universe he rules.

No one has expressed the pain and unfairness of this world more poignantly than Job; no one has voiced disappointment with God more passionately. We must still attend to Job's complaints and God's fierce response. But the Book of Job begins not with the complaints—the human viewpoint—but with God's point of view. In the prologue, the scene of the wager establishes a darkly shining truth:

Job—and you and I—can join the struggle to reverse all that is wrong with the universe. We can make a difference.

The Book of Job gives no satisfying answers to the question, "Why?" Instead, it substitutes another question. "To what end?" By remaining faithful to God through his trials, Job, cranky, cynical old Job, helped transform the very pain and unfairness of this world that he had protested so vigorously against unto a treasure of timeless truths for us to harvest.

The Road Less Traveled, by M Scott Peck, opens with a blunt, three-word sentence. "Life is difficult." If reduced to a single sentence, the Book of Job would express something similar, for the loud cry "Life is unfair" resounds from almost every page. Unfairness is no easier for us to swallow today than it was for Job thousands of years ago: consider the most common curse word in the English word: God-damn. People say it not only in the face of great tragedy but also when their cars won't start when a favored sports team loses when it rains on their picnic. That oath renders an intuitive judgment that LIFE ought to be fair and that God would somehow "Do a better job" of running the world.

We tend to think that life should be fair because God is fair. But God is not life as we think of life. And if I confuse God with the physical reality of life, by expecting constant good health, for example, then I set myself up for a crashing disappointment. God's existence, even his love for me, does not depend on my good health. If we develop a relationship with God APART from our life circumstances, then we may be able to hang on, despite all the unfairness of life. Isn't that the main point of Job?

Most of the Biblical heroes: Abraham, Joseph, David, Elijah, Jeremiah Daniel, went through trials, much like Job. For each of them, at times, the physical reality surely seemed to present God as the enemy. But each managed to hold on to trust, hope in Him despite the hardships. In doing so, their faith moved from a "contract faith" (I'll follow God if he treats me well) to a covenant relationship that could transcend any hardship, cut, or wound.

Jesus offered no immunity, no way OUT of the unfairness, but rather a way through it to the other side. And as the psalmist stated, "When thou walkest through the valley of the Shadow of Death; Thou is with me. My friend, you are walking through, unto life again." The Cross of Christ may have overcome all evil, but it did not overcome unfairness. For that, Easter is required. Someday, God will restore all physical reality to its proper place under his reign. Until then, it is a good thing to remember that we live out our days on Easter Saturday.

The apostles' faith, as they freely confessed, rested entirely on what happened on Easter Sunday, when God transformed the greatest tragedy in all history, the execution of His son, into a day we now celebrate as Good Friday. Those disciples, who gazed at the cross from the shadows, soon learned what they had failed to learn in three years with their leader. When God seems absent, he may be closest of all. When God seems dead, he may be coming back to life. God is with you right now, where you are, and as you are. There is no tree cut too deeply that the scent of rain cannot cause purpose, passion, and life to bud again. There is hope for a new beginning when your life feels at an end.

The three-day pattern-cycle: Tragedy, Darkness, Triumph, became for New Testament writers a template that can be applied to all our times of testing. We can look back on Jesus, the proof of God's love, even though we may never get an answer to our "Why" questions. Good Friday demonstrates that God has not abandoned us to our pain. The evil and suffering that afflict our lives are so real and so significant to God that He willed to share them and endure them himself. He, too, is acquainted with grief and sorrow. On that day, Jesus himself experienced the Silence of God—it was Psalm 22, not Psalm 23, that he quoted from the cross. Jesus, the Tree of Life, was cut like no other "tree" was cut. And Easter Sunday shows that in the end, suffering will not triumph. Therefore, "consider it pure joy, whenever you face trials of many kinds," writes James, and "in this you greatly rejoice, though now for a little while you may have had to suffer grief in all kinds of trials," writes Peter; and "we also rejoice in our sufferings, " writes Paul. The apostles go on to explain what good can result from such "redeemed suffering"—maturity, wisdom, genuine faith, perseverance, character, and many rewards to come.

Why rejoice? Not for the masochistic thrill of the trial itself, but because what God did on Easter Sunday on a large scale he can do on a small scale for each of us. The afflictions addressed by James, Peter, and Paul would likely have ignited a major crisis of faith in the Old Testament. But New Testament writers came to believe that, as Paul expressed it in Romans 8:28 ', all things work together for good.' As Joseph stated it so well in regards to the deep cut of betrayal from his brothers: "What you meant for evil, God meant for good."

16

That well-known passage is often distorted. Some people interpret its meaning as "only good things will happen to those who love God." Paul meant just the opposite, and in the very next paragraph, he defines what "things" we might expect: trouble, hardship, persecution, famine, nakedness, danger, sword. Paul endured all those. Yet, he insists, in all these things, we are more than conquerors; no amount of hardship can separate us from the Love of God. It's just a matter of time; Paul says that before you smell the scent of rain! Just wait—God's miracle of transforming a dark, silent Friday into Easter Sunday will someday be enlarged to cosmic scale.

God gave unto Job his own personal "summer's purse," called a "Man Bag," in the form of the natural scent of rain, which ignited the spark of hope resulting in new buds of purpose, passion, and life again as seen at the end of Job's days. I smell the scent of rain. You can too. Hope in God.

"My hope is built on nothing less than Jesus Christ, His righteousness; I dare not trust the sweetest frame but wholly live on Jesus's Name." William Batchelder Bradbury (1816-1868)

CHAPTER 3

Hope for a Tree, Hope for Me!

For there is hope for a tree if it is cut down, that it will sprout again, and that its tender shoots will not cease. Though its root may grow old in the earth, and its stump may die in the ground: YET through the SCENT of Water (RAIN), it will bud and bring forth branches like a plant. (Job 14:7-9, NKJ version)

Have you ever wondered why the writer uses the image of a tree to convey hope unto all those who have been "cut," and feel as if their very vitality, their sap, their life has wasted away and withered up?

Wonder why throughout the scriptures, men and women were often compared to "trees?"

Have you ever wondered why in Psalm 1, the very detailed picture of the blessedness of God upon people is seen through the imagery of a tree that is planted by the rivers of water?

Throughout the culture of the day, people were very keen on the value of trees to their livelihood. The Bible contains more references to trees and wood (over 525) than to any other type of living organism except humans. The references of trees are found from the very first book of the Bible, which contains a reference to the Tree of Life in the Garden of Eden (Genesis 2:9) to the last book of the New

Testament, which refers to the Tree of Life as a major feature in Paradise (Revelation 22:2,14).

Trees provided tremendous natural benefits to those who lived among them. Trees provided shade, food, and fiber for people. Trees were a source of oil and proved useful for animal feed, wood, fuel, and construction.

Because of the importance of food, cutting fruit trees during the siege of an enemy town was prohibited. (Deuteronomy 20:19-20)

Trees were very much utilized to make utensils, as noted in several chapters of Exodus. Early in the Bible, trees are mentioned as a source not only of food but also of beauty (Genesis 2:8). The beauty of trees is also a theme in the Song of Solomon.

In a sense, the message of the Bible can be summed up by the symbolism of four trees. The first was the Tree of Life in the paradise of the Garden of Eden (Genesis 3:22-24). This became the tree of the knowledge of good and evil (the second tree), of which Adam and Eve ate the fruit, causing the fall (Genesis 3:4-6,17-18). Third, Jesus' cross is referred to as a "tree" and is linked to Deuteronomy 21:22-23. "If a man guilty of a capital offense is put to death, and his body is hung on a tree, you must not leave his body on the tree overnight. Be sure to bury him that same day, because anyone who is hung on a tree is under God's cures." In the Christian doctrine of salvation, Jesus is taking the curse, removing the cures of the tree of good and evil, and leading to the fourth and last tree: the Tree of Life in the paradise of God with "...leaves of the tree...for the healing of the nations. No longer will there be any curse" (Revelation 22:1-3).

In what does the writer of Job attend unto his hope for the tree? The tree is cut, the sap has spilled out, and vitality is vanquishing. The air is dry, and the heat is hot. Hope?

What would cause a tree that is cut, that, for all general purposes, is void of value, outwardly wasted away, and empty of any fruit, begin to put forth new shoots, begin to give evidence that something is working on the inside being now seen on the outside? For verdant green shoots to sprout out from the very place in which there were apparent death and dryness?

The Scent of Rain:

19

The only hope of a tree that was cut and withered away was to wait for the east wind to blow. And you, my friend, are called to be "trees"—oaks of righteousness as seen in Isaiah 61:3; "they will be called oaks of righteousness, a planting of the LORD for the display of his splendor." Your time will come; you will experience the scent of rain if you do not grow weary and faint. The source of the scent of rain is the God of the whirlwind and the east wind.

There is yet HOPE, as stated in Job 14:7-9:

"For there is hope of a tree if it is cut down, that it will
sprout again, and that the tender branch thereof will not
cease. Though the root thereof waxes old in the earth and
the stock thereof die in the ground: YET through the scent
of rain, it will bud, and bring forth boughs like a plant."

There is yet hope for a tree; there is yet hope for ME! And also, see Proverbs 13:12: "Hope deferred makes the heart sick, but a longing fulfilled is a tree of life."

The human spirit needs hope to survive and to thrive. One expert said, "Since my early years as a physician, I learned that taking away hope is for most people like pronouncing a death sentence. Their already hard-pressed will to live can become paralyzed, and they may give up and die. Doctors in World War II, Korea, and Vietnam said some prisoners died from the condition of what they called 'give-up-itis.' And what they meant by that is if prisoners faced grim conditions with no prospect of freedom, and some of them became demoralized, and some of them became mired in despair, and after a while they became apathetic, and they refused food and they refused to drink, they would spend their time in their bunk just staring into space. With their hope drained away, these prisoners eventually just wasted away, and they died. They died of give-up-itis."

Perhaps you are reading this today, or perhaps you know of someone who is suffering from give-up-itis. You have already given up your dreams—your desires, that once burned bright and clear—have now faded back into your memory as hope deferred. Your marriage, your financial dreams, your business careers, your family hopes, all seem to have either been placed on hold or disconnected from reality.

God has an antidote for the give-it-up-itis and its give-it-over-itis. Give it over to God. Cast all your cares upon Him, for He cares for you. Trust in the Lord with all your heart and lean not unto your understanding. Your way, your own predetermined time by which God needs to answer your prayers will not lead you out of your prison of shame, self-condemnation, guilt, and remorse. God has provided a way, a deliverer, a rescuer, a healer, a savior, a redeemer a friend, a comforter, and a life management manual that contains all the instructions and guidelines for you and me to live in a godly manner that is, first, pleasing to Him, and second, beneficial to you.

I don't know your pain, your shame, loss of purpose, the decline of passion, the vitality of life, but one thing I do know is that God, your God, is a God of HOPE!

Romans 15:13 describes God as the God of Hope. In total, there are 95 references to hope in the Old Testament. There are another 85 references to hope in the New Testament. The theme of hope is woven throughout scripture, and it's going to be the dominant thread that is woven within the tapestry of your life. God is hope. God is in you as hope. You have hope because God is in you. Greater is He that is in YOU than he that is in the world.

Hopefully, there will be moments while you are reading this book that the sweet-smelling fragrance of the scent of rain will permeate your senses and subconsciously or consciously, the light of hope will peer through the shadows of sadness, sorrow, shame, and uncertainty, clearing your path to hope again!

There is yet hope for a tree. Though it is cut, at the scent of water, it shall bud and live again!

Allow me to be quite clear what I mean by hope, by drawing light unto what I definitely do not mean. I am not speaking of the **Poor Trio Substitutes for hope**: Wishful thinking, Blind optimism, and Ambitious dreams. **Wishful thinking is when we try to hope things in or out of our life.** We blow candles on our birthday cake and say, "I hope I have another year of health and happiness."

Or we turn on the TV and say, "I hope the Boston Red Sox will win the World Series again."

Blind Optimism is another kind of hopeful attitude. Although being an optimistic person is a great quality, it can be quite disastrous to see everything through rose-colored glasses. Everything. These kinds of people paper over their problems as if they didn't exist. They avert their eyes from the ugliness of the world. To them, everything is fine all the time. Ask them how they are doing, and they reply "GREAT - just great!" when internally, they are experiencing the most severe spiritual drought within their soul.

Sort of like the sign on the bulletin board at the grocery store. "Lost. Dog with three legs, blind in the left eye, missing right ear, tail broken and recently castrated. Answers to the name Lucky." You can call that dog Lucky all you want. That is not a lucky dog. And sometimes people in their blind optimism will pretend things are great when they're not. That's not biblical hope.

Third, a poor substitute for hope is perhaps what has been my learning edge. Ambitions, dreams—these are the lofty goals we tend to set right before we enter a new year, or after attending a conference on "Leaders and their Vision," or after hearing a minister speak on the importance of following "God's Call or Dream for Your Life." All of that is fine. It's wonderful to set ambitious goals and then to work toward achieving them. The problem is that often; we are restricted by our limitations or by things that are outside of our control. Corporate restructuring, natural disasters, accidents, physical setbacks, unplanned pregnancies, surprises by associates, and friends abandoning agreed-upon dreams and plans previously, all of these are just some of the ways our ambitious goals can be deferred.

But sometimes our limitations or circumstances or other people can affect our dreams. Our dreams can be derailed or temporarily detoured, especially when we are cut as the tree in Job 14:7-9. When we are cut, in such a way that we end up disappointed or worse, we give up, like the child in the mall who refuses to walk any more: "Daddy, carry me—I can't walk."

The Trio of Poor Substitutes for hope cannot sustain, reclaim, regain one's purpose, passion, hope, and life again in every season of life. However, in contrast, God's hope can and God's hope will sustain and reclaim your purpose, passion, and life again—when you can smell the scent of rain.

Allow me to contrast, wishing thinking, blind optimism, and ambitious dreams with biblical hope. For most people, hoping is something that they do. But the Bible talks about hope as something we have. See the difference. Hope is something you have. You can possess it. You can own it. You can grab hold of that rope, tie a knot, and hold on. For someone who is a follower of Jesus Christ, here is the definition of hope. Hope is the confident expectation that God is willing and able to fulfill the promises that He has made to you.

Hebrews 6:19 says, "We have this hope as an anchor for the soul firm and secure. Our hope is only as good as what it is attached to. What or whom would your hope be attached to?"

My hope is built on nothing less than Jesus Christ His righteousness; I dare not trust the sweetest frame but wholly lean on His sure name; on Christ the solid rock I stand; all other ground is sinking sand; all other ground is sinking sand. Hope in and of itself has no power. You can wish for something, you can hope for something, you might feel a little better about it. We might even fool ourselves into thinking everything is ok. But the only way hope has any real power is when it's anchored in the God who has real power. And not only real power but a real desire out of His love for you to help you. Those who follow Jesus Christ hope in the confident expectation that God is willing, and God is able to fulfill the promises He's made to them.

The storm you may presently be in today could cause your heart and soul, your very stomach to toss and to turn-like riding the "Space Mountain" ride in Orlando, and, as Psalm 107 says, you are mounting up the heavens and descend crashing down to the very depths of the sea-your Heart is melting. Your soul seems to be slipping even away from you. You feel as if there are moments, even days, where you are "losing your mind." My friend, it is in these moments of all moments that one must smell the scent of rain and hope again! Sing again—know that the anchor of hope still holds, in spite of the storm.

Read the following stanza, repeat them often, allowing them to be the refreshing fragrance of the scent of rain unto you today.

The Anchor Holds by Ray Boltz

I have journeyed
through the long dark night
out on the open sea
by faith alone
sight unknown
and yet his eyes were watching me

CHORUS
the anchor holds
though the ship is battered
the anchor holds
though the sails are torn
I have fallen on my knees
as I faced the raging seas
the anchor holds
in spite of the storm

I've had visions
I've had dreams
I've even held them in my hand
but I never knew
they would slip right through
like they were only grains of sand

CHORUS

I have been young
but I am older now
and there has been beauty these eyes have seen
but it was in the night
through the storms of my life
oh that's where God proved his love to me

There are two areas of hope which are especially relevant unto one who is in a season of "drought, dryness, despairing of life, little if any passion, no wind in one's sails" (the doldrums of life) deadened unto their pain and other peoples pain, discouraged by the delay upon delay, disenfranchised by the "in crowd" due to the perceived or real faults, fumbles, and flaws on one's life.

First, we have hope because we're absolved of our past. Our past is past. Our past has no power over our present unless we permit it to. The Blood of Christ is better than bleach.

Lamentations 3:21: "This I call to mind and therefore I have hope. Because of the Lord's great love, we are not consumed for His Compassions, never fail." They are new every morning. What the writer is saying is that we can live with hope as followers of Christ because even though we may fail God (which we all do) and even though we may fail our children in some way (which we all do) and even though we may fail our spouse in some way (which we all do) even so God's compassion, His forgiveness, His absolution for those wrongs we've done in our past is a renewable resource. It is never exhausted. It is fresh, and it is available every single day as the fresh morning dew.

Within the game of golf, one of the very first new terms I learned, and one of my favorite words was "mulligan." I can still remember the first hole and tee which I was on in which this term was given to me by the one who taught me golf. Swing, swoosh, and...the slightest connection possible between club and ball caused the ball to trickle inches from where I had hit it. How did that happen? With all my force and focus...inches? My colleague smiled as he looked at me, saying, "go ahead and get a mulligan."

"Mulligan? What's a mulligan?" I asked while shaking my head.

"A second chance," he replied. "Go ahead, pick up the ball, and place it back on the tee-try again."

A mulligan is a "do-over," a second chance. Wow—now golf was more exciting to me than ever before! I loved mulligans. I thanked God for mulligans. Every Hole that day had a mulligan awaiting me! Mulligans! Do-overs!

Some people need a do-over from God because of guilt. Like when you squeeze the toothpaste out of the tube, guilt has just squeezed hope out of your life. That's what guilt does. Guilt lies to us, and guilt tells us, "You are disqualified from a do-over. You will never get a clean slate. Guilt squeezes hope from our lives. Hope is like the fresh scent of rain—it has it's own power to wipe away the stain of shame and soften the pounding pain within your heart so you can sing again.

Isaiah 61:7 tells us that instead of shame and confusion, God will give you joy and bless you double for your trouble. The second cause for hope is that we are assured of a good future and bright hope

25

Jeremiah 29:11: "For I know the plans which I have for you, to give you a future and a bright hope." Right now, your future may not "look bright"; all you may see is the clouds of chaos and confusion; The trials, tests, and temptations which you are experiencing may be encircling you, enshrouding you with thick darkness—fear has gripped your heart—you don't know how, if it's at all possible, you'll ever come out and see the "light again."

In your daily darkness, discouragement, despair, and dryness of soul—hope in God.

Remember the immutable, irreversible, irrefutable facts:

"God is present with you. Right now, right where you are, God will not abandon you. God will help you. God is with you in your trouble." (Psalms 46:1)

God loves you. God is NOT angry with you and trying to get "even" with you. One of the most important activities which will awaken and ignite your ability to smell the scent of rain, the fragrance of Heaven, is for you to praise Him in the storm. To turn your eyes upon Jesus, to look full in His wonderful face, and the things of this world will grow strangely dim in the light of His glory and grace. As you give ATTENTION and INTENTION to focusing upon God and who He is to you, your ability to "smell" will awaken: celebrating what is right will awaken your smell sense unto His presence, power, peace, and provision.

I'll Praise You in the Storm

I was sure by now
That You would have reached down
And wiped our tears away,
stepped in and saved the day
But once again, I say, Amen and it's still raining
As the thunder rolls, I barely hear Your whisper through the rain,
"I'm with you."
And as Your mercy falls, I raise my hands
And praise the God who gives and takes away
And I'll praise You in this storm, and I will lift my hands
For You are who You are no matter where I am
And every tear I've cried
You hold in Your hand
You never left my side and though my heart is torn

What do you do when you've been "cut," and your spiritual "sap" has slipped away, drained out? What do you do when you've recognized that you're in a "spiritual slump?" We all go through dry spells. We all will have seasons of valleys and wilderness where we Do NOT feel spiritually alive, where we don't feel close to God when our prayers are bouncing off the ceiling. We feel disconnected from God. We feel like David in Psalm 71: "O God, do not be so distant from me." We all go through these dry spells, and we recognize that we're not as close as we used to be to God.

When you're going through a dry spell, when you're going through a spiritual slump, you don't lose your salvation. But you do lose the joy of it. You lose happiness. You lose the peace. You lose confidence. You lose the closeness that felt to God. And you feel kind of dry and empty and dusty inside. What do you do when you've lost your spiritual vitality? What do you do when you've lost your cutting edge?

The answers to the above questions are going to be answered in the following pages.

But first and foremost: Place your HOPE In GOD! Declare with me today. Say it out loud. Agree with me that "There is yet hope for a tree for me. Though I am cut, though, I have lost my spiritual vitality. At the scent of rain, it will—I will—bud again, Flourish, bear forth fruit again, I will reclaim my purpose, passion, and life again. I smell the scent of rain!"

Expect God to give you back what has been lost. This is the faith step. I must believe that God can and will and wants to bring a new beginning when life feels at an end. I've got to have faith; I've got to expect Him to give me back what I've lost. I've got to believe that God will heal what I'm willing to reveal. I've got to believe that God will restore.

I know that it seems humanly impossible: I've seen the old "dead" stumps within the deep northern Maine forests as the trees were cut down by the logging companies. I've walked the muddy dirt roads with my Dad during hunting season, walked over rows and rows of cut down logs, and observed "death" all around me...only a year to two later, while hunting within the very same territory, been shocked to see green everywhere—sprouts of life growing from within the very "dead stumps!"

That which was once thought "dead" had from within it the very essence of life growing up amidst it! There is yet hope for a tree. Though it is cut, at the scent of rain, it will bud again. There is yet hope for a tree; there is yet hope for me, I smell the scent of rain.

What seems impossible in your life? I'll never feel that I belong. I'll never feel valuable again. "I'll never be close to God again." You're wrong. "I could never be blessed by God. You don't know what has happened in my past." You're wrong. "I could never be used by God. I could never have His power in my life. I'm just one tiny person, insignificant." You're wrong. "I could never see God pour out His grace, His strength, His mercy, His power, His presence in my life because I've really messed up my life. That can't happen to me. It's impossible." You're wrong.

Jeremiah 15:9: "The Lord says, 'If you return to Me, I will (not hope, not might, not I'll think about it) restore you so you can continue to serve me!'

What a promise! Remembering God's promises and reaching out to God, requesting God through faith to send "the rain" will create the atmosphere within your heart, soul, and mind to receive, perceive the scent of rain—God's favor to flourish again.

Don't quit believing. You're too legit to quit. You can make it. Hope deferred makes the heart sick, but a longing fulfilled is a tree of life. Today as you smell the rain by increasing hope, faith, and love, the stem of new passion, purpose, and life is beginning to grow.

In Mars Hill Full Gospel Assembly my 'Scent of Rain' Pastor was Mark Dunfee and as a young teenager, I must have sung this song a thousand times. I'm so glad Brian Cumming as our worship leader sang it a thousand times, for it finally found its way in and became indelibly lodged within my heart and mind as an unshakeable truth. "You can make it...you can make it. This trial you're going through God's going to bring you through—you can make it. You can make it, I don't know what's going wrong, but God won't let it last too long, cause you're not in this thing alone—you can make it."

At the scent of rain, there is yet hope to bud again!!

I Have This Hope

by 10th Avenue North

As I walk this great unknown
Questions come, and questions go
Was there a purpose for the pain?
Did I cry these tears in vain?
I don't want to live in fear
I want to trust that You are near
Trust Your grace can be seen
In both triumph and tragedy
I have this hope
In the depth of my soul
In the flood or the fire
You're with me, and You won't let go
But sometimes my faith feels thin
Like the night will never end
Will You catch every tear?
Or will You just leave me here?
But I have this hope
In the depth of my soul
In the flood or the fire
You're with me, and You won't let go
So, whatever happens, I will not be afraid
Cause You are closer than this breath that I take
You calm the storm when I hear You call my name
I still believe that one day I'll see Your face
And I have this hope
In the depth of my soul
In the flood or the fire
You're with me
I have this hope
In the depth of my soul
In the flood or the fire
You're with me, and You won't let go
In the flood or the fire
You're with me, and You won't let go

CHAPTER 4

The Science Behind the Scent of Rain

"Petrichor is the natural scent produced when rain falls on dry soil.

Petrichor (pronounced /ˈpɛtrɪkər/; from the Greek word, *Petros*, meaning "stone" and *ichor* being the name of the scent of rain on dry earth. Ichor now refers to any watery discharge from a wound or inflammation.

Petrichor is the name of the scent of oil, released after rain on dry earth, though it may be called the essential oil of earth or rock oil. One may also regard it as the blood of the earth, released after rain. It has been found that petrichor is a complex mixture of more than fifty distinct chemical compounds. It should have an agreeable odor and in concentrated form, produce perfume.

During rain, the oil is released in the air along with another compound, geosmin, producing the distinctive scent. Geosmin may be called the vitamin of the earth. Geosmin, which literally translates to "earth smell," is an organic compound with a distinct earthy flavor and aroma, and is responsible for the earthy taste of beets and a contributor to the strong scent that occurs in the air when rain falls after a dry spell of weather (petrichor) or when soil is disturbed.

The term was coined in 1964 by two Australian researchers, Bear and Thomas, for an article in the journal *Nature*. They created the word from two Greek stems: *Petros* (stone) and *ichor* (in Greek mythology, the substance that flowed through the veins of the gods). In the article, the authors describe how the smell derives from an oil exuded by certain plants during dry periods, after which it is absorbed by clay-based soils and rocks. During rain, the oil is released into the air along with another compound, geosmin, producing the distinctive scent'.1

Allow me to paraphrase the meaning of petrichor to the common street language, which I so readily appreciate as well: **Petrichor is the scent of fresh rain after it has fallen on the dry earth.**
"Petrichor, as the scent of fresh rain, can only occur when the combination of multiple factors collides with each other. Oil from the earth—rocks, any clay substance or vegetation—whether seen by the human eye or not seen, is emitted from its clay source or vegetation and released into the atmosphere wherein it collides with Geosmin.

Geosmin does nothing besides exuding the smell. For inexplicable reasons, human beings are extremely sensitive to it. If you have a trillion liters of water and ten liters of geosmin in it, the human nose would still detect it. That's about a 100,000 to a million times more sensitive than we are to any other substance. That's why even if there's very little of that in the soil when you lift a clump of warm earth, you would smell the geosmin in the air."2

Fascinating? Wow! The scent of rain is the fragrance resulting from the release of oil from within rock, clay or vegetarian and earthly surfaces that ascends upward and collides, meets together, (agrees with) with the water droplets descending and upon impact—or union together—the two separate elements produce a NEW compound called petrichor—the scent of rain!

CHAPTER 5

Job and the God of the East Wind

"The Mediterranean eastern coast region is marked by two major seasons: summer (hot and dry) and winter (rain) with two shorter interchange periods that mark the transitions from one to the other. The weather systems involving wind are of two kinds, one coming from the northwest and bringing rain, the other, sirocco—a hot, dry wind coming from the southeast. The two shorter interchange periods are so-called because they are marked by alterations between the eastern, hot, and dry winds and the western, rain-bringing winds. Plowing and seeding take place during the last stages of the winter season. The end of this season is marked by the onset of the east wind whose heat kills floral vegetation (Isaiah 40:6-8), and with its accompanying dust, air pressure, and other features make life unpleasant and sometimes cause illness and even death. For about fifty days, the two weather systems alternate, and then they subside into the long hot, dry summer. In the spring interchange, then, the east wind carries negative connotations.

But in the fall, the east wind carries quite a different message. Its first emergence signals the end of the hot, dry summer and the coming of the first rains from the west. In one observation, a first fall east wind was followed within two hours by a heavy ten-minute rain accompanied by thunder and lightning, and this, in turn, was followed two or three hours later by the return of the east wind. It is as the east wind awakens the west wind and brings the west wind at the beginning of the year where New Year's Day comes in the fall, the east wind is good.

With this imagery in mind, our eyes are alerted for meteorological imagery in the chapters which follow, and we are not disappointed. Without attempting to trace this theme in all its occurrences, we may note its appearance in Job 9:17-18, where Job complains, "He crushes me with a tempest and multiplies my wounds without cause; he will not let me get my breath but fills me with bitterness." Throughout the dialogues, Job and his friends frequently employ images of water and fertility on the one hand and desecration and wilderness on the other. And Elihu, who goes on and on almost endlessly in his youthful attempt to inform his elders of his own "inspired" insights finally, in celebrating God's wisdom and power, speaks of God's activity in the weather that brings rain, thunder, and lightning. (36:24-33) Elihu becomes so caught up in his description that it is as though he actually experiences the onset of such weather in which (as in Psalms 29) he hears the thunder of God's voice (37:2-5), followed by rain (37:6). During this description of the awesomeness of such weather, he pauses to say, "Whether, for correction, or his land, or love, he causes it to happen" (37:13).

Imagine with me that the long discourses we read in Job between himself and his friends are actually conversations stretching over the long hot summer. His intermittent hopes arise as longing for the smell of the scent of rain (Job 14:7-9), but his final self-description leaves him still in scorching misery (30:29-31)." 1

G od did answer Job but not at first as Job thought he would answer. God answered Job in and by the rain. God spoke first through natural events, and so it often is with you and me, although sometimes it's difficult for us to discern and hear what He is saying.

"God's answer does not plunge him into the mire. God has not rendered him mere dust and ashes. This, I take, is what Job means in 42:6 as he recants what he has charged God with, and he is comforted concerning his miserable state as set forth so poignantly in Chapter 30. What lies before him, as he witnesses the renewal of the earth, is the possibility that he might have the wish expressed so wistfully in Chapter 29 simply, a return to the ordinary goodness of life." 2

He who had briefly hoped for the scent of rain now experiences it, in and through the renewal of the natural world as the fall winds brought the downpour of rain so long-awaited for.

Though he is none the wiser as to how to explain his experiences, he is renewed in his appetite for purpose, passion, and life.

The Scent of Rain—Essence of Hope has the purpose of awakening. Revive within you the areas which have wilted, perhaps wasted, and withered away under the incessant scorching heat of life's pressures, pains, brokenness, betrayals, and burden. God himself is faithful, He alone is faithful, and He is more than able, He is willing to send the rain to blow again so that what man may have written off—and perhaps even signed your epitaph—YOU SHALL LIVE AGAIN.

"The Bible says even the righteous shall fall seven times, but He rises again!" (Micah 2:9). The Bible says I may be knocked down, but I'm not knocked out!

As the final words of the book have it, in the end, Job dies old and satisfied with life. God sent the rain to satisfy the waste and desolate land: God gave Job double for his trouble! I trust God will do the same for you. Job 38: 25-27 on life-giving rain in the wilderness:

"Who has cleft a channel for the torrents of rain, and a way for the thunderbolt, to bring rain on a land where no man is, on the desert in which there is no man; to satisfy the waste and desolate land, and to make the ground put forth grass."

"So Job apparently felt about his life, for in 30:14, he had described himself with the images of a city under attack by those who had breached its walls and rolled on amid the crash of its walls and buildings. The result was to leave him abandoned in a wilderness inhabited only by wild creatures such as jackals and ostriches (30:29-31). But it is precise to such a region that God's rain comes. To what purpose?

The NSRV reads, in 38:27, "to make the ground put forth grass." But the Hebrew word behind "ground" is, again, a particular term: *mosa*, meaning a source, place of coming forth, place of producing. God's rain comes to turn that dry, drought-stricken wilderness (as in Jeremiah 2:6) into a source of lush vegetation, food for all the wild grazing animals and birds that roam within it (Job 39:1-18).

It is when Job has entered deeply into the wilderness of his experience, in a no man's land devoid of the marks of human habitation, human meaning-making, that Job finds the rain, for which he, like a felled tree, had earlier in Chapter 14:7-9 expressed a wistful longing." 3

And in a much smaller way, I realize it is when I have been willing to let go of what has been lost: position, possessions & yes even people, that I create the open space for a new future to emerge even better than I had imagined. When I recognize that the scaffolding of my past is no longer necessary for my future it is then that to the extent that it does happen, I experience the transformative power of *The Scent of Rain—Essence of Hope* to turn this barren, drought-stricken human servant, against all the odds, into a source, or rather a channel, of a word that others may find helpful and life encouraging.

Right now, right where you are, lift the eyes of your heart unto the God of the whirlwind, the God of the east wind, for He will surely send the rain. God will satisfy your longing soul and fill your heart with goodness. My friend, God, will send water upon him that is thirsty. He will send floods upon the dry ground, and the desert, barren wasteland areas of your life will blossom as the Garden of the Lord. God's delays are not His denials. Where God places a comma, let no man place a period. God is never late, but He sure will cause us to sweat!

Let us pause and ponder the following previous points. Everyone like a tree will experience pain, cuts, loss. Job discovered the strikingly similar parallel between the natural cycles of wind and rain relating to a tree towards his personal experience, resulting in "smelling the scent of rain" to reclaim His purpose, passion, and life again.

Job's end was better than his beginning; he discovered the "bend in the road" was not the end of the road unless he failed to make the turn. My friend, today you are taking the turn around your bend and though you have been cut, yet there is hope—at the scent of water, you will bud again.

It is God's will to send the rain, so I can "smell the scent of rain," and hope again—live again!

Key Question:

How does one navigate themselves through the seasons of transitions successfully to revive, renew and awaken their appetite for the life their inwardly long to live, the love they intensely seek to experience, and the liberty they internally crave? The answer to that question will be aptly discussed throughout the remaining chapters.

In my formative years within Mars Hill Full Gospel Assembly, Brian Cumming would sing the following song. And 30 years later, the song still reverberates within my soul and gives me hope that I can smell the scent of rain:

"It's beginning to rain, rain, rain in the voice of my Father-; saying Whosoever will come drink of this water; for I promised to pour my Spirit out on your sons and your daughter; if you're thirsty and dry; lift your hands to the sky; it's beginning to rain."

CHAPTER 6

Scriptural Sources of the Scent of Rain

Rocks, earth, and vegetation are the primary sources from which the scent of rain is derived from. You and I are like Peter, "little stones." In Matthew 16, Jesus is speaking straight into the identity and destiny of Peter, his disciple who just earlier had verbally expressed His radical realization and declaration of "who exactly was the man named Jesus." As Peter declared the infamous statement: "Thou are the Christ, The Son of the Living God!" What a watershed moment, a defining moment, a moment not of intellectual breakthrough or scientific discovery but spiritual revelation! So what does Jesus say unto Simon in return?

Jesus speaks immediately, wasting no time in drawing attention and intention, not unto Himself, but back onto Simon. Jesus says the familiar words in Matthew 16:7-18: "And Jesus said to him, 'Blessed are you, Simon Bar-Jona because flesh and blood did not reveal this to you, but My Father who is in heaven. I also say to you that you are Peter, and upon this rock, I will build My church; and the gates of Hades will not overpower it.'" The word for "Peter" in Greek is *Petros*, which means "a little stone," but Christ said He would build His church upon another rock—in the Greek: *petra*, a large rock. What Jesus meant by the contrast between the large and small rock was that Peter was one of the stones in the church (I Peter 2:3-5), but that Christ Himself was the foundation stone (I Corinthians 3:11).

Peter is the little stone while Christ is the rock. The difference is distinguished in the Greek wording. Christ had surnamed this Simon Bar-Jona in John 1:42:

"And he brought him to Jesus. And when Jesus beheld him, he said, Thou art Simon the son of Jona: thou shalt be called <u>Cephas, which is by interpretation, a stone</u>." Peter himself understood what Christ meant. He knew that <u>Christ was the only foundation stone</u> and that he, and the rest of God's chosen ones, were little building blocks upon that foundation. I Peter 2:5-6: "Ye also, <u>as lively stones</u>, are built up a spiritual house, a holy priesthood, to offer up spiritual sacrifices, acceptable to God by Jesus Christ. Wherefore also it is contained in the scripture, Behold, I lay in Sion a chief cornerstone, elect, precious: and he that believeth on him shall not be confounded."

Yes. He that believes in Christ as the Son of God will not be confounded! Today you may not have clarity regarding your next step; you are uncertain about your future, perplexed about the mounting pressures within and without yet you are NOT confounded. Confounded is NOT WHO you are. You and I are the children of God, you and I are lively stones, and our identity and destiny are in Christ and come from Christ. No one can ever take that away from you; try as they might. When my path is dim, and sight is short, darkness obscuring my way. I may feel confounded; however, who I am is NOT my experience nor my feeling. I am a living stone whose very openness and wounding produces the necessary elements from which in due season, I will smell the scent of rain and see again.

As lively stones, you and I have the oil and geosmin within and upon us awaiting the set time, the "kairos moment" whereby God turns our mourning into dancing, disappointments into appointments with the miraculous, hurts into halos, setbacks into setups and your pains into gains through the scent of rain.

Secondly, water (atmospheric) in the heavens is another primary source of the scent of rain—petrichor. Water is the symbol of the Word of God applied to the soul, in power, by the Spirit of God. It is seen in the book of Isaiah 55:10-11: "As the heavens are higher than the earth, so are my ways higher than your ways and my thoughts than your thoughts. As the rain and the snow come down from heaven, and do not return to it without watering the earth and making it bud and flourish, so that it yields seed for the sower and bread for the eater, SO IS MY WORD that goes out from my mouth; it will not return to me empty, but will accomplish what I desire and achieve the purpose for which I sent it!"

It is also in Ephesians 5: 26, where we find the water definitely identified with the Word in the expression, "The washing of water by the word." God's Word reveals his will. Within the Word of God, one will find the will of God. The Bible states, "He sent His Word and healed them and delivered them from all their destructions"—Psalm 107:20. God has the Word waiting for you. One word from God can change your life. When you place your faith in His word to your life right now in your new situation, you are enabling God's Word to work within you. God's word works.

What we see as rain falling upon the ground was, at one point a form of water invisible to the eyes. Faith can see the invisible to do the impossible. As in creation, the waters covered the earth above and beneath, so God's Word is always available unto those who seek His Word with all their hearts. In the types, water has as large a place as the blood. Both flowed from the pierced side of the Lord Jesus in death as the point of a spear ruptured his physical heart—out flowed water and oil. Dr. Stroud, in his book, explains that the death of Christ resulted because His heart ruptured. He reasons that the blood passed from the heart into the pericardium or caul of the heart where it collected into a red clot (blood) and into the limpid serum (which he calls "water"). Therefore, after Jesus was dead, says this doctor, a spear was thrust into His side and out flowed a little blood and water which had collected around His heart (John 19:34). So, it is reasoned along with the shedding of all His blood, Jesus died of a broken heart! The Tree of Life was wounded and cut; however, through his stripes, we are healed.

As such, Jesus Christ truly is the supreme scent of rain and the essence of hope unto all humankind. He is the most petrichor person who ever walked this earth. His Words were and are life; He brought hope to whoever reached out to him, and He is the same yesterday, today and forever, He is forever and always the ultimate scent of rain.

The old chorus says it best: "Jesus, Jesus, oh Jesus: there's just something about that name. Master, Savior, Jesus, like the fragrance after the rain, kings, and kingdoms shall all pass away, but there's something about that name."

A Satisfied Thirst

The following excerpt comes from *Bold Love* by Max Lucado. The story that follows is from *Chapter 2: A Satisfied Thirst:*

"Mommy, I'm so thirsty. I want a drink." Susanna Petrosyan
heard her daughter's pleas, but there was nothing she could

do. She and four-year-old Gayaney were trapped beneath tons of collapsed concrete and steel. Beside them in the darkness lay the body of Susanna's sister-in-law, Karine, one of the fifty-five thousand victims of the worst earthquake in the history of Soviet Armenia.

Calamity never knocks before it enters, and this time, it had torn down the door.

Susanna had gone to Karine's house to try on a dress. It was December 7, 1988, at 11:30 a.m. The quake hit at 11:41. She had just removed the dress and was clad in stockings and a slip when the fifth-floor apartment began to shake. Susanna grabbed her daughter but had taken only a few steps before the floor opened up, and they tumbled in. Susanna, Gayaney, and Karine fell into the basement with the nine-story apartment house crumbling around them.

"Mommy, I need a drink. Please give me something."

There was nothing for Susanna to give.

She was trapped flat on her back. A concrete panel eighteen inches above her head and a crumpled water pipe above her shoulders kept her from standing. Feeling around in the darkness, she found a twenty-four-ounce jar of blackberry jam that had fallen into the basement. She gave the entire jar to her daughter to eat. It was gone by the second day.

"Mommy, I'm so thirsty."

Susanna knew she would die, but she wanted her daughter to live. She found a dress, perhaps the one she had come to try on and made a bed for Gayaney. Though it was bitter cold, she took off her stockings and wrapped them around the child to keep her warm.

The two were trapped for eight days.

Because of the darkness, Susanna lost track of time. Because of the cold, she lost the feeling in her fingers and toes. Because of her inability to move, she lost hope. "I was just waiting for death."

She began to hallucinate. Her thoughts wandered. A merciful sleep occasionally freed her from the horror of her entombment, but the sleep would be brief. Something always awakened her: the cold, the hunger, or, most often, the voice of her daughter.

"Mommy, I'm thirsty."

At some point in that eternal night, Susanna had an idea. She remembered a television program about an explorer in the Arctic who was dying of thirst. His comrade slashed open his hand and gave his friend his blood.

"I had no water, no fruit juice, no liquids. It was then I remembered I had my blood."

Her groping finger, numb from the cold, found a piece of shattered glass. She sliced open her left index finger and gave it to her daughter to suck.

The drops of blood weren't enough. "Please, Mommy, some more. Cut another finger." Susanna has no idea how many times she cut herself. She only knows that if she hadn't, Gayaney would have died. Her blood was her daughter's only hope.

"This cup is the new covenant in my blood," Jesus explained, holding up the wine.[1]

The claim must have puzzled the apostles. They had been taught the story of the Passover wine. It symbolized the lamb's blood that the Israelites, enslaved long ago in Egypt, had painted on the doorposts of their homes. That blood had kept death from their homes and saved their firstborn. It had helped deliver them from the clutches of the Egyptians.

For thousands of generations, the Jews had observed the Passover by sacrificing the lambs. Every year the blood would be poured, and every year the deliverance would be celebrated.

The law called for spilling the blood of a lamb. That would be enough.

It would be enough to fulfill the law. It would be enough to satisfy the command. It would be enough to justify God's justice.

But it would not be enough to take away the sin, because the blood of bulls and goats can't take away sins. Sacrifices could offer temporary solutions, but only God could offer the eternal one.

So he did.

Beneath the rubble of a fallen world, he pierced his hands. In the wreckage of a collapsed humanity, he ripped open his side. His children were trapped, so he gave his blood. Jesus Christ was cut—as no other man was or would ever be cut—on Calvary's Cross, so that you and I might be made whole, healed, restored, so that the dead, barren, empty places within our lives can "live, bud again" and as such, there is yet hope for a tree...

It was all he had. His friends were gone. His strength was waning. His possessions had been gambled away at his feet. Even his father had turned his head. His blood was all he had. But his blood was all it took. "If anyone is thirsty," Jesus once said, "Let him come to me and drink."

Admission of thirst doesn't come easy for us. False fountains pacify our cravings with sugary swallows of pleasure. But there comes a time when pleasure doesn't satisfy. There comes a dark hour in every life when the world caves in,, and we are left trapped in the rubble of reality, parched and dying.

Some would rather die than admit it. Others admit it and escape death.

"God, I need help."

So the thirsty come. A ragged lot, we are bound together by broken dreams and collapsed promises. Fortunes were never made. Families that were never built. Promises that were never kept. Wide-eyed children trapped in the basement of our failures.

And we are very thirsty. Not thirsty for fame, possessions, passion, or romance. We've drunk from those pools. They are saltwater in the desert. They don't quench—they kill. "Blessed are those who hunger and thirst for righteousness..." We thirst for heaven's rain for the Premier Petrichoric Person—for Jesus Christ—for He is our hope of glory. We thirst for the scent of rain again.

Righteousness. That's it. That's what we are thirsty for. We're thirsty for a clean conscience. We crave a clean slate. We yearn for a fresh start. We pray for a hand which will enter the dark cavern of our world and do for us the one thing we can't do for ourselves—make us right again.

"Mommy, I'm so thirsty," Gayaney begged.

"It was then I remembered I had my blood," Susanna explained. And the hand was cut, and the blood was poured, and the child was saved.

"God, I'm so thirsty," we pray.

"It is my blood, the blood of the new agreement," Jesus stated, "shed to set many free from their sins." And the hand was pierced, and the blood was poured, and the children are saved." 1

And so even as this natural earth so often "thirsts" for the "blood of the earth" for the scent of rain, so sun-scorched African plains and Texas fields can be transformed into vibrant, verdant vegetarian and life-producing fields. So our hearts and our lives, within the wilderness, heat, and arid atmosphere, yearn desperately for His touch, His presence, to "light our fire again," for in His presence, there is the fullness of joy, and at His right hand, there are pleasures always. We thirst first and foremost for Him, the ultimate scent of rain. He has promised that He will satisfy the thirsty heart and fill the longing soul with goodness.

The third substance of the scent of rain is oil, which is emitted from a "wound," an opening or upon a rock-earth or vegetational surface. Most Christians regard oil as a symbol of the person and ministry of the Holy Spirit. Throughout the Old Testament, we see oil being used for holy purposes. The priests were consecrated and ordained unto God as oil was poured upon their heads: "Then shalt thou take the anointing oil, and pour it upon his head, and anoint him" (Exodus 29:7 - see also Leviticus 8). During such ceremonies, oil was used abundantly, for it ran down the priest's beard and clothing: "It is like the precious ointment upon the head, that ran down upon the beard, even Aaron's beard: that went down to the skirts of his garments" (Psalm 133:2). The kings of Israel were also anointed with oil as they took up office. David, the King of Israel, declared in perhaps the most famous Psalm of all, Psalm 23:5: "you anoint my head with oil, my cup runneth over!"

Just as you and I are "lively stones," so you and I all have "oil" within us, we all have an anointing. In John, Chapter 2:26-27, John writes to the Church: "These things have I written unto you concerning them that seduce you. But the anointing which ye have received of him abideth in you."

John states that we, the Church, we the believers, have an anointing. He says in Verse 20 of the same chapter: "But ye have an unction from the Holy One, and ye know all things." The words unction and anointing are the same Greek word. It speaks of pouring or smearing on or an application of oil and, of course, that speaks of the unction or the anointing of the Holy Spirit.

My most fragrant, the freshest smell of the scent of rain, brought "purpose, passion, and a meaning for living," as mentioned earlier in Chapter 1. The scriptural passage of Luke 4:18 was as fragrant unto the "nose of my heart" as any natural fragrance—it was the most beautiful fragrance I had ever known. I knew from that day forward that indeed I had been anointed. The Bible said it, so I believed it. Faith turned my "night" into the day...until the clouds of doubt and the **dismal performance of my first public speaking experience in Zion Bible Institute also known as North Point College.** One of the requirements within the public speaking class as a sophomore was to compose and present a biblical "sermon" in front of my peers. The date had been given to me, and being the severe student that I was, my preparation was more than sufficient, my confidence was sky-high, and excitement was bursting within me. The day had come in which I could "display" my anointing!

Oh, the foolishness of youth! The text of my first sermon in front of my class would be Psalm 61:1-3: "Hear my cry, O God, listen to my prayer. From the ends of the earth, I call to you (little did I know to what ends-I would be led unto.) I call, as my heart grows faint; lead me to the rock that is higher than I. For you have been my refuge, a strong tower against the foe." I was so excited—thrilled—to deliver my message and boy, was it going to be great! Like a horse sprinting out of the gate, my introduction was fluid, forceful, and felt as if I was hitting my stride until suddenly, a freezing moment came upon me unawares, uninvited, and in mid-sentence. I froze, saying nothing and spontaneously burst out in tears. I couldn't finish "the race." I stopped short and in excruciating embarrassment step aside from the podium and sat down, still crying. My sophomore sermon fell flat as teardrops flowed down my face.

Talk about not feeling anointed! I bombed it! For weeks following my message meltdown, I struggled with unanswered questions "If I'm called to preach the Gospel, how can I do this if I can't even conclude a message without falling apart and crying?" Questions such as "If I was so anointed, how come I failed miserably and in front of my class? Where was God in that?" constantly nagged within my heart and were slowly drowned out by the constant chatter of homework, social life, and school deadlines. And then came spring.

CHAPTER 7

The Day of the Oil from My Fingertips

It was a midweek spring evening in 1987 during final exams of my sophomore year, weeks before I would fly to Malawi, Africa for my first missionary trip, that I found myself within Zion's chapel attending a prayer service. The prayer meeting had started with hundreds at 7 p.m., had now filtered down to a dozen or more by 9. Lights were dimmed, doors were shut, and a sweet, sweet presence filled the room as we pressed further in prayer. In a hall seating hundreds, there was plenty of room for students to lay themselves on the floor, kneel, walk between the aisles, sit or stand while praying, and this night, all of it was going on.

I had been walking about praying, then stopping to raise my hands upwards while reciting scriptures and praising God until I stopped. I felt the "freezing" feeling again; however, it was a warm one—the suddenness and immediacy of the "warm feeling" flowing from my head unto my hands were unmistakable, and so I stopped to pay attention, to give attention to what at the moment became "surreal." I opened my eyes and instantly lifted my hands upwards chest high, open-palmed, and looked at my hands. Oil, tiny drops of oil were on my fingertips. I wiped the oil droplet of a fingertip, and immediately a new oil droplet surfaced. Amazing. Instantly my spirit and mind raced backward in time to replay Luke 4:18: "The Spirit of the Lord is upon me because He hath anointed me to preach the gospel to the poor." Could this be a sign of the "anointing?" I admit I wanted to believe that it was. I needed to believe that it was, that I was truly anointed, however just as fast as the thought came to me of Luke 4:18, came a second and very different thought crashing through my mind, stating: "You're making this up, it's just sweat." And so I looked again—and no, it was not sweating; it was a yellowish oily substance forming on the tips of my fingers. Without wasting any more time and in a sincere attempt to distinguish fact from fiction, I, amidst the waging doubt and adrenaline rush, walked up to a colleague of mine, Lori Fortier—now Lori Potutschnig. "Lori, look. Do you see what I see?"

She took my hand, looked at it, and said, "that's oil, Eric. You're anointed. Why don't you lay your hand on my head and pray for me?" And so I did, just as soon as I laid my hand on her, she graciously slipped onto the floor, continuing in prayer.

I looked around me, and said to myself, "in the presence of 2-3 witnesses, a matter is established" and walked unto another colleague, Michael Spencer. "Mike, look—what is it?"

Mike looked and said, "That looks like oil, man. You're anointed. Put that hand on me." And so I did, and Mike, like Lori, lay on the floor.

For the next hour, it was as if the scent of rain -the essence of hope was flowing forcefully through the ceiling ducts within the chapel. I felt God, as if I was electrified, the scent of rain revived purpose, passion, and life again. Malawi, Africa, there was a harvest to be reaped, and if ever I was prepared to go, it was now with the anointing.

The first chemical compound within the scent of rain is oil flowing, leaking, emitting from the pores of rocks and vegetation, which mostly occurs within and following seasons of high intense heat, dryness, and drought. As living rocks and like the tree in Job 14:7-9, regardless of our shape or size, the field we are planted in or the measure of our fruitfulness, how young or old we are, there will be seasons and times that we are cut. From within us flows fear, pain, residues of regret, and emissions of negative emotions, and at this time, we are open either unto obstacles or opportunities, unto our hurt or our healing, unto our pain or our gain, unto our fear or faith. For were we to look closer within, we would see and believe that the oil, which represents the Holy Spirit, has never left us. The Holy Spirit abides within us and works amid our wounding, ascending through us and will work for us causing all things to work together for our good.

Think it not strange, the fiery trial which is to try you as though some strange thing has happened unto you, although your circumstances and situation are hard for you to explain. You can smell the scent of rain.

Geosmin has been called the "earth's vitamin," and you and I have been made from the dust of the ground. Geosmin is a universal chemical compound, and I propose to you today that within you and I lies the inherent, immutable, indefensible ability to HOPE AGAIN!

Paul stated in II Corinthians 1:21: "Now he which establisheth us with you in Christ, and hath anointed us, is God." We see that John, the Beloved Apostle, said that we, as believers, have an unction, and now we see that Apostle Paul says the same thing. Wherever we are, in whatever season we are in, the "oil" of the Holy Spirit is within you and I. That is a fact. Anything you feel or think contrary to this is just that: a feeling and a wrong belief. You have an anointing. God gave it to you, not man. There will be plenty of days in which you do not "feel anointed" or see the "oil" within or upon you...however, don't give up heart. You will bud again through *The Scent of Rain—Essence of Hope*.

CHAPTER 8

Cuts, Wounds, and Scars

Hast Thou No Scar
by Amy Carmichael

Hast thou no scar?
No hidden scar on foot, or side, or hand?
I hear thee sung as mighty in the land,
I hear them hail thy bright ascendant star,
Hast thou no scar?

Hast thou no wound?
Yet, I was wounded by the archers, spent.
Leaned me against the tree to die, and rent
By ravening beasts that compassed Me, I swooned:
Hast thou no wound?

No wound? No scar?
Yet as the Master shall the servant be,
And pierced are the feet that follow Me;
But thine are whole. Can he have followed far
Who has no wound nor scar?

H umpty Dumpty sat on a wall, and Humpty Dumpty had a great fall, all the king's horses and all the king's men, couldn't put Humpy back together again. However, the King could: if only He would and He should.

Now perhaps you're sitting securely upon the wall of your life, marriage, business, and ministry. All is well. The admiration of many as they pass by your wonderful "wall" soaks pleasantly within your soul as the rising morning sun. Life is good. It could be better, but you're not going to complain, at least not yet. If you're sitting securely, then this book might be of secondary help, but to your co-worker, friend, spouse or neighbor, pastor, or peer, *The Scent of Rain—Essence of Hope* is of primary importance because they've gone literally "off the wall."

Yes, you've known a number of them, and perhaps you've even been an anonymous inductee of the "off-the-wallers." Humpty Dumpty is our founder and friend. We, as followers of Humpty Dumpty, have fallen off of our "wall." We lead with our limp. To the naked eye, one might not be able to recognize an "off-the-waller" within a crowd of hustling walkers in downtown Manhattan or within a crowded Macy's but to the observant, to the one with an open heart, open mind, open will, the universal sound of an "off-the-waller" screams silently—yet soundly—as two grey whales.

We "off-the-wallers" walk with the same limp, speak with similar sounds and feel with humble hearts, the pain, pressures, problems, and perplexities of others. For us, as they have all been cut, wounded, and scarred. We've been cut relationally, cut in our ministry, cut in our career through broken promises, betrayals, and saboteurs. Cuts are excruciating painful—they hurt whether we see the cut coming or whether we have not seen the cut coming, cuts hurt. Plain and simple. Cuts stink. Wouldn't it be nice to leave life without cuts? Pain, disappointments, heartache. I know that I would—if I could.

Every tree (that's you and me) will be cut, if not more than once in their life. I have, and so have you. Yet there is hope for a tree when it is CUT—at the scent of rain, it shall bud again. Everyone will be cut—it's a when, not an if—it's not if you will join the ever-growing tribe of "off-the-wallers" so much as it's how you will join (better or bitter) hopeful or helpless, and when you will join, and when you enter that unexpected, unfamiliar, unwanted tribe. Allow me to be the first one to welcome you with a warm heart, hearty hug into a guilt-free zone:

- What do you do when you're cut, when your life and dream seems to be all going "down the drain?" Smell the scent of rain.
- What do you do when you're cut, and shame has left its searing stain? Smell the scent of rain.
- What do you do when you're cut, and your passion has grown passive in ways you just can't explain? Smell the scent of rain.

- What do you do when you're cast violently into chaos, turbulent transition, and deeply feel the pounding pain? Smell the scent of rain.

Throughout the next several pages, we are going to walk through the hallways of a hospital to view the before and after photos of one who has personally been there-and because he has been there, you as a visitor could well possibly be the recipient of some encouragement and enlightenment that hopefully would alleviate your incessant insecurity, throbbing heart pain, and stomach-churning chaos enabling you to face your future with HOPE, Persevere and Pass-through your Present season into Experiencing the all restoring, healing, cleansing, renewing, aliveness of the scent of rain.

> *I declare unto you today that though you are cut-You will smell the scent of rain, and your passion, purpose, and life you will reclaim. Before I open the windows unto you of some of my past wounding and show you my scars of past cuts, allow me to share from personal experience the purpose and principles of our cuts, wounds, and scars, so we can learn how to profit from our cuts, wounds, and scars, to discover how to transform our pain—to transmit it into gain—how to smell the scent of rain when all you see is wounded, damaged goods, and feel worthless, as if you'll never experience the sweet life again.*

For there is hope for a tree if it is cut down, that it will sprout again, and that its tender shoots will not cease. Though its root may grow old in the earth, and its stump may die in the ground: yet through the scent of water, it will bud and bring forth branches like a plant. (Job 14:7-9, NKJ version)

Life without cuts and scars? Impossible. Learn from your cuts and scars? Hopefully. Your cuts and scars make you more human, more touchable, more real, more authentic, more compassionate, and more caring. Your cuts and scars are the indications that the frailty of life, evil, and the human condition have had an impact on you. Your cuts and scars make you sensitive. They also make you credible. There is a wounded healer who is known by His cuts and scars—how about you?

No one can revive hope within the masses until first they feel the pain within the individual. The many are in the one. The pain is tied to the unfulfilled dreams and objectives that never have had the opportunity or permission to live. Touch the pain, and you touch what really matters. Speak to the root of that pain and let the scent of rain awaken hope, and the sprouts of a new day emerge as life from the dead.

Richard Rohr has been as the scent of rain and the essence of hope unto my life in his many writings. He has taught me the following:

"1. The cut one is always the one with the gift; the comfortable one knows nothing about it.

The word "innocence" (innocent) "not cut-wounded yet: is not a complimentary term in mythology. The "puer" is the young man who refuses to be cut, or more exactly, refuses to recognize and suffer cuts, wounds that are already there. He's just going to remain nice and normal so that everybody will accept him. In our culture, he might smugly remain white and middle class, healthy, "sinless" Catholic, Protestant, pretty and happy, maybe even drive a classy car or wear the latest clothing.

He refuses to let it fall apart. He refuses to be cut, wounded, much less to allow the humiliating cuts and wounds to be sacred and sanctifying. Yet, I believe that the Gospels are saying there is no other way to know something essential.

2. Allowing our always unjust cuts and wounds to become sacred cuts and wounds, is the unique Christian name for salvation.

If there is one consistent and clear revelation in the Judeo-Christian Scriptures, it is that the God of Israel is the one "who turns death into life" (see Deuteronomy 32:39, Romans 4:17, 1 Corinthians 1:9), when we can trust the transformative pattern when we can trust that God is IN THE SUFFERING. Our cuts become sacred cuts, and the actual and ordinary life journey becomes itself the godly journey, trusting God to be in all things, especially in suffering.

Paul states this mystery even more clearly in Galatians 2:20: "I have been crucified with Christ (the small self and false self) must die...and I live now not with my own life (it feels utterly inadequate and now unnecessary), but with the life of Christ who lives in me (realization of an Indwelling gratuitous Lover)."

We, as humans, so often fight, deny, resist, and disbelieve anything that we feel unready for, or unworthy of. Thus Jesus had to present the gift in the image of a resented banquet in Luke 14:12-24. Paul speaks in the language of free inheritance for those who would prefer to be slaves (Romans 8:14-17) In all cases, it feels like a wounding to our sophisticated soul. For some strange reason, love wounds us, and beauty hurts us.

When the cuts happen in a secular society like ours, we usually look for an immediate way to resolve it, playing the victim, mobilizing for vengeance, or looking for someone to blame. A sacred culture-sensitive to the Spirit individual would never bother with such charades and missed opportunities. Rather than a sacred cut, suffering for us becomes a minor cut and, eventually, an embittering wound. As such, Paul warned against such as in Hebrews 12:15: "Look after each other so that none of you fails to receive the grace of God. Watch out that no poisonous root of bitterness grows up to trouble you, corrupting many."

Rather than a sacred cut, suffering for us often becomes a mere cut and, eventually, an embittering wound. The journey stops there, and there's no FUTURE! Without the dignifying cut, there is no mystery, no greatness, no soul, and surely no Spirit. The theme is so constant in poetry, literature, and drama, that one wonders how we could continue to miss it.

What we have now in the West, by and large, is embittering wounds. The spiritual "machine" for turning cuts into "crowns" has been lost by people. Yet all the mythologies and mystics tell us that WE WILL BE CUT, WE MUST BE CUT. It is what we do with the CUT that makes all the difference. There is something that you know after you have passed through the "night sea journey" (Psalms 107:23). They that go down to the sea in ships—that do business in deep waters—these see the works and the wonders of the Lord.

I've learned that faith allows one to trust that God is in the suffering and trial: "I thank you, Lord, for what you want to teach me in this." Now you won't say that probably on the first day, nor did I, or probably on the second day, but maybe on the THIRD DAY! And believe me, if you hold fast to the confession of your faith without wavering, you will indeed experience a THIRD DAY, in which you will be resurrected! Such people are indestructible, or in Christian language, "being born again," and it has more to do with having come through suffering ALIVE, and better, than having an emotional experience after an altar call.

Ancient religions called it such an experience as "the inexorable wheel," the mystery of life and death that just keeps turning. You have to take your time on the downside of the wheel and take your turn on the upside of the wheel and learn in both cycles. That's why Jesus said the rich man could not know what he was talking about (Mark 10:26) because the "rich man" refuses to take his turn on the downside of the wheel. He tries to buy his way out of absurdity, to avoid the essentially tragic nature of human existence, by manufacturing a false path of comfort and control. Nothing new happens here. Nothing is transformed. The Holy One is not trusted. The self remains small—Jesus is not lifted. Our old self is.

Dying is not extraneous to life; it is a part of the mystery. And you do not understand life until you stand under death. Yet both sides of the mystery must be experienced, and it is my experience that more often than not, one is more easily accepting the life part than the death part of Christianity. The resurrection-overcoming, victory themes are so highlighted that one fails to experience in practical, meaningful, measurable means the very victory, life that they speak of, simply because they fight against—resist, run from anything which even smells of death.

Yet both sides of the mystery must be experienced. The Eastern religions speak of the yin and the yang, while nature religions simply speak of darkness and light; the Jewish people speak of slavery and deliverance; we Christians speak of death and resurrection. But we are all pointing to God's universal pattern of trust and transformation. This is rightly spoken of as being "reborn" but has less to do with an emotional Church experience than "a realigning life experience." Yes, God is in all things. God is in the dying as well as God is in the living. God rises in all things. And both at the same time." 1

The scent of rain is precipitated by an opening of the spores from the oil, which resides upon or within vegetation, clay, and rocky surfaces. With that in mind, one must understand that part of the steps one must take to smell the scent of rain is to a) acknowledge your cut, your wounding. God can only heal what you reveal, and b) embrace your wounding and its inflammation, perhaps even the daily discharges which occur by being cut open.

1. The Cut of "Abandonment"—the Aloneness, and Feelings of Being "Forgotten" Emits a Foul Fragrance Which is Tattooed Upon the Senses of One's Memory

She lay dying upon an old aluminum hospital bed in the summer of 1993 in Romania. All 75 lbs of her, rocked in constant pain of cancer, killing her blood cells and ferociously eating her life as if there was no tomorrow. We had admitted her to the hospital just days earlier after stumbling into her shack of a home 14x12 space, wherein she laid upon a black encrusted mattress upon a wooden floor, having not walked or bathed in months. Her boy, Christie, serendipitously knocked upon our Romanian apartment door one ordinary morning. Christie was doing his daily routine begging for bread, day after day, so that he and his mother could live. But on that day, the scent of rain and the essence of hope fills his nostrils. My wife Marianne invited him in, handed him an orange, which he began feverishly to eat, orange peel and all until Marianne took the orange back to peel it, gently instructing him on how to eat an orange. It was the first orange this 12-year-old had eaten.

Within two hours of meeting Christie, we drove him to where he said he lived alone with his dying mother, Cassandra. She lay there motionless, her eyes opened, and upon seeing Marianne, she grimaced in pain and said, "you are an angel." We gently carried her into our vehicle to get her some medical attention; meanwhile we had her 14x12 shack completely scrubbed and sanitized as best as possible. Marianne personally bathed her and lovingly removed her hair lice.

Daniel and Marianne took on the responsibility for her care, including having her admitted to a hospital only to see her after several medical examinations discharged for there was nothing that they could do to help her. She died shortly thereafter and was given a proper burial leaving Christie orphaned.

Cassandra, for the three weeks in which we serendipitously met her, had, for the first time, experienced the fresh scent of rain—heaven's rain. Unconditional love, non-solicited, non-judgmental. Her eyes opened brightest and clearest the day in which she willingly accepted Christ as her Savior and was baptized ever so gently by Daniel in a bathtub.

Christie was alone, numbed by the events surrounding the sickness and slow death of his only living relative, his mother. And so, Christie was adopted by Walk in the Light Ministries, Ilie Coroama (Ilie Coroama is my father-in law) founder of Walk in the Light Ministries and became the first of more than 200 children adopted in Romania.

The cut of being abandoned—forgotten—brings with it genuine emotional feelings of pain. At that moment, it's time to smell the scent of rain. In the Desert of Delayed Prayers of Waiting in the Wilderness, the Desert of Doubt, and Discouragement, you will be tempted to believe that God has forgotten you. Have you ever been forgotten? Perhaps you drove to a meeting, waited, and waited and waited, but they never showed up? You were shown up!

Cut: Forgotten, and it hurts. It's embarrassing.

2. Malawi, Africa, January 1989

I had invited one of my best friends, Stephen Potuschnig, to return with me to my first mission love—Malawi, Africa. Steve said, yes! With great excitement, we began planning and preparing to leave in January 1989 for three months of a great adventure. Two young men, 20 years old, engaged to beautiful women, were leaving the shores of the great U.S.A. to preach the Gospel and serve the people in Malawi, Africa. I was thrilled to be taking my best friend Steve, if not a little proud, to be taking him to the people and places I had been before on my first trip there. Throughout the 18-hour plane ride, I was sharing with Steve stories of my earlier African experiences and speaking highly of the host missionaries whom we were about to meet "Wait until we meet them. They're real revolutionaries for Jesus—no namby-pamby cotton candy Christians— they're the real deal!"

As the African 30-seater plane descended into Blantyre, Malawi, the sunset was lowering, leaving the African landscape in breathtaking beauty. Butterflies of excitement rose within my heart, back into Africa—wow, again—and with my best friend! "I can't wait to meet Rodney. I've heard so much about this revolutionary from Mike—this is gonna be just great!"

Being in no great hurry, Steve and I climbed last out of the plane, walked across the tarmac into the airport's luggage-holding area, where soldiers were standing guard, rifles strapped across their chests. This is not Maine or Pennsylvania. It's always a heart-throbbing time when your eyes are viewing the luggage turntable, watching and waiting to see whether your luggage actually made it! It would be a long three months without it!

Yes, one luggage and a duffel bag filled with a tent, supplies, etc., and another set for Steve. Luggage arrived—Africa, we are ready. Here we come! We then turned to walk out of the airport luggage area, on past the gates where people were waiting for friends and family to exit the airport.

Now, when you're waiting for someone to pick you up whom you have never met or known, there are some familiar pick-up patterns. The host who is picking up the passenger holds up a piece of cardboard or paper with the name of the airplane on it or the hostname. The passenger, while exiting the departure area, is glancing around to all the faces with a look on his face "Are you the one, or should I look for another?" as the disciples of John the Baptist said to Jesus: "Are you the one or should we look for another?"

When the above two practices do not bring the desired results—being remembered, found, connected, and picked up—then the tired, exhausted airplane flyer does the third thing. Wait, stand, and wait for the host to arrive to pick you up. And so Steve and I waited. And waited and waited and waited.

We waited, watching each fellow passenger exit the arrival area unto the smiling, friendly faces of those who picked them up. Do you know what that looks like? Broad smiles open arms. "Glad to see you! How was your trip? I love you!" Well, Steve and I waited...and waited until there was no-one. No-one left around but ourselves.

In disbelief, with great embarrassment sitting in my stomach like a rotten potato, I said to Steve, "perhaps they're just late, surely they wouldn't have forgotten us!" And so we waited and waited until the sunset dropped beneath the horizon, the lights that were on in the airport began to turn off, and policeman began to usher Steve and I out of the airport, closed the gates, and locked them. Steve and I were left outside of the airport gates in Blantyre, Malawi. Darkness had descended, and no-host missionary had arrived. We had been forgotten: a rotten feeling.

What do you do when you've been forgotten? Left outside of the airport gate after 18 hours of international travel? You're mentally drained, physically exhausted, emotionally upset, not to mention hungry, and in need of a shower! What do you do when you're being forgotten? Move forward.

I said to Steve, "Let's go."

Steve said, "Where are we going?"

I said, "I don't know, but we can't stay here, on the side of the street alongside this airport gate! It's after 10 p.m. and dark. We gotta find a hotel."

And so we hailed a taxi, asked to be taken to the town of Blantyre, and we walked, looking for a hotel, motel, anything that had a room in it. Long story short—we ended up in a dingiest, dirty, open space, living in a hotel that was more like a brothel.

Lying awake on the minuscule mattress, amidst a cement floor with no door in the room, other than beads descending from the ceiling to the floor, on two beds, there lay Steve and I.

First night in Africa: Forgotten. Where was Rod? How could this have happened? Didn't he get the message that we were coming? Doesn't anyone answer the phone? What are we going to do in the morning? Where are we going to go? We didn't get much sleep, and at the crack of dawn, we were out the door—instead, through the stringed beads—and walking down the streets looking for a payphone.

Fortunately, within my little black book of addresses was a pastor whom I had ministered with and met on my first trip to Malawi. A telephone number as well! Wonderful—a phone call was made, a friendly voice on the other line, and soon four wheels were quickly on their way to pick up Steve and I. We hopped happily into a Jaguar, of all vehicles! Picked up in style—with a friendly pastor who gave us a friendly embrace!

"Come to my home. So glad you could visit with us." The pastor's home was a huge spacious, beautiful home—abundance was evident—and quickly, a buffet of delicious, colorful fruit was placed before us for breakfast. Wow. God's Plan B sometimes is better than your Plan A!!

Steve and I remained with the Blantyre pastor for two days, and upon the third day, Rod was contacted and reluctantly received Steve and I. Talk about NOT starting on your best foot! Thus the re-entry into Africa—into Malawi—did not go exactly as we had planned. Our host had forgotten the dates and times of our arrival leaving us abandoned, forgotten, feeling unwanted all in a third world country as mere youths.

What may your experience be like of being forgotten, of being "abandoned," of sensing the shame of not being "wanted?" For a pastor, it is the vote of no confidence at the annual church business meeting, a notice of dismissal. For a husband or wife, it is the email left opened on a laptop or phone revealing an affair or divorce papers received in the mail.

I have a friend who, upon returning from a ministry trip home, was eager to walk into his house and greet his wife with a kiss. Upon entering the door, he viewed his home stripped of furniture; all of his wife's clothes and personal belongings were gone as well as the kids. Abandoned. Rejection. It sucks. It's real. Whatever fashion or means by which it happens—its pain is ever-universal and unrelenting.

I understand your pain of being cut—believe me, I do. I've lived the emotional experience in which the Psalmist speaks so much about, in whose words I've found a soulmate. David cried out in his cuts and wounds. Psalms 22:1-2: "I am forgotten as a dead man out of mind. I am like a broken vessel." Can he be any clearer? Can there be a lower hole than that?

Psalms 142:4: "No man cared for my soul." Perhaps there are no sadder six words than that. No man cared for my soul. Loneliness is perhaps the greatest risk to a healthy life. Science has proven that we are created to belong to something, connect to someone other than ourselves.

Perhaps you feel that you're in a present experience of a desert—parched and dry. You're in a very long, very hot drought of unanswered prayers. The discouragement has settled in, you're wilting, withering, and wasting inwardly away due to the absence of "rain," of conscious awareness of purpose, passion, and life. Do you feel forgotten?

My friend. God has not forgotten you! He knows exactly where you are, what you are going through right now, and He is monitoring every step along your path. But we are just like the children of Israel who doubted God's daily care for them, even though prophets were sent to deliver wonderful promises from Heaven. God's people sat in darkness, hungry and thirsty, praying for deliverance and comfort. God bottled every tear, and He heard their cry and answered, "I will preserve thee... You shall no longer hunger and thirst... I will have mercy on you and lead you by springs of living water... for the Lord will comfort his people and have mercy on all the troubled ones..." (Isaiah 49). Did Israel rejoice in these promises sent directly from the throne of God? Did God's people quit their fretting and begin trusting in the Lord to see them through? Did those who were hurt and confused believe a single word of these promises? No!

"But Zion said, The Lord hath forsaken me, and my Lord hath forgotten me" (Isaiah 49:14).

These were not reprobates or sons of the devil. Instead, they were those "who sought the Lord... the sons of Abraham... those who knew righteousness... in whose heart was the law of God..." How much clearer must God make His Word to his children? God was greatly concerned because they were not appropriating or hearing His promises. You can almost sense the impatience of the Lord in rebuking their unbelief. "I, even I, am he that comforteth you: who art thou, that thou shouldest be afraid of men... and forgettest the Lord thy maker, that hath stretched forth the heavens, and laid the foundations of the earth; and thou hast feared continually every day because of the fury of the oppressor as if he were ready to destroy..." (Isaiah 51:12-13).

Is it that we can't hear Him? Perhaps for those who have never heard the words of our loving, faithful compassionate Father God—yes, Romans 10 clearly states, "How can they believe if they have not heard?" Hearing precedes believing.

What about those who have heard, have gone to Bible school, attend church services, sing in the choir, serve in the church and community? What about them? How is it that we who have heard and do hear have a tough time trusting in the tough times of dancing in the dark, singing through our struggles?

Perhaps it is as my experience has taught me the following. The voices of fear, cynicism and judgment are screaming, shouting in our pain so loudly that until we learn how to mute the volume of such voices, the gentle ever so soothing calming assuring voice of our comforter the Holy Spirit will not be heard to the point where we smell the scent of rain and hope again.

In our pain, when we are wounded and cut ever so deeply, we easily ignore and forget God's promises! Does it all sound familiar? Here we are today as the children of the same Heavenly Father, having in us the glorious promise of the Holy Ghost's comfort—yet we go about daily fearing the oppressor. We know what our Lord has promised us: guidance, peace, a shelter from the storm, a way where there seems to be none, a supply for every need, healing for every hurt. Do we believe in any of them? Do we just put these promises out of our minds and go on our way, worrying and fretting and taking matters into our own hands? I'm afraid so! And we are all alike. We get in a tight place, a desert, wilderness place; we get lonely and depressed; we fall into temptation and yield to lust; we make tragic errors and live in guilt and terror, and through it all, we choose to forget all that God has promised us. We forget we serve a God who laid the very foundations of this earth. We forget our Father is all-powerful, and that he made all things that exist. We see only our problems. Our fears and pain, like a cataract, shut out the vision of His power and glory. We get afraid; we panic; we question; we doubt. We forget in our hour of need that God has us in the palm of His hand. Instead, like the children of Israel, we are afraid we are going to blow it all and be destroyed by the enemy. How difficult it must be for our loving Father to understand why we won't trust Him when we are down and in need. God must think to Himself, "Don't they know I have gravened them upon the palms of My hands... I could no more forget them in their hour of need than a mother could forget her suckling child... and even though a mother could forget her child, I cannot forget a single child of mine" (Isaiah 49:15-16).

My friend, God has not, cannot, and will not ever forget you. He cares for you, and He is forever faithful. He is watching over you even when you feel as if no one cares, no one is there. He is with you.

3. The Cut of a "Dream"

It was the spring of 1999 when a missionary, while on furlough, ministering in a church, that he was asked by the existing pastor to consider changing course in mid-air, to be the pastor of the very church he had spoken in an hour earlier. "I know that you are returning to Romania, I understand your vision and passion, but I have to ask you this question: Would you consider being our pastor?"

Placing his fork away from the steak which he had been eating, the missionary glanced at his wife with a twinkle in his eye and said: "I told you so."

The missionary's "I told you so" came because the day earlier the missionary had spent the afternoon meeting Pastor John—the acting pastor—for the first time at one of the homegroup leader's homes, and after answering questions regarding Romania and his mission, while in the car returning to their guest home, the missionary commented to his wife: "I feel that tomorrow Pastor John is going to ask me to be the pastor of the church. Yes, he's going to ask me over lunch."

The missionary's wife said, "you're crazy, what makes you think so?"

The missionary said, "I just feel it here." He pointed to his heart. "I smelled the scent of rain."

The scent of rain is the freshest fragrance after a long dry spell. Like the summer showers which come out of nowhere, they pour torrential rain for a few minutes, and then the clouds pass away, leaving the fragrance of rain to be smelt. So it was that Saturday afternoon when the missionary first smelled the fragrance of "rain," a new flood of purpose, passion, and life was flowing. Energy and creativity at full speed. A new cycle change, a new launch, and a new chapter was being brought written.

Sometimes the rain comes suddenly, and seemingly out of nowhere, clouds quickly appear that were not on the horizon before and before one can prepare themselves and pick up an umbrella or put on a coat, the RAIN FALLS—and boy does it fall—and then the fresh scent of rain appears.

Ending a very long chapter of international mission-evangelism to assume the pastorship of a church known as being a church alive as opposed to being dead was an oxymoron. For indeed there was "death in the pot," as in the story of Elisha, and things really weren't as they at first appeared.

However, when God calls you when He serendipitously surprises you by His Spirit, He often conceals what you later wish He'd revealed. But had He, you may have never said "Yes." So He allows by His wisdom what He could have prevented by His power. Thankfully, God did reveal unto the missionary while on an Air France flight to the States to visit the church in July, prior to assuming the pastorate in September a life-altering, life-changing passage of scripture: Job 14:7-9:

> For there is hope for a tree if it is cut down, that it will
> sprout again, and that its tender shoots will not cease.
> Though its root may grow old in the earth, and its stump
> may die in the ground: yet through the scent of Water
> (RAIN), it will bud and bring forth branches like a plant.
> (Job 14:7-9, NKJ version)

This became unto the missionary his life message. At first, he received it as speaking unto the church, which he had known was deeply cut like a tree, yet as each year passed, he slowly understood that the "tree" was not all about "them" the tree was also about "him."

The missionary had spent his previous 12 years, since he was 20, ministering to the children from within the garbage dumps of Mexico city to the abysmal, horrendous Romanian orphanages (some of which Diane Sawyer documented) to the Malawian and Mozambique refugee camps, to the recently liberated and newly formed youth churches behind the torn Iron Curtain in cement jungles (cities and apartment projects) of St Petersburg, Russia, Romania, and Ukraine, to lepers and bible school students and the lowest caste of India, to the Vienna college students. Knowing Christ and making Him known was his purpose, passion, and life. It was all about people. Not programs nor products, not buildings or banks, but people.

The church had suffered some very serious piercing—it was cut severely and only the Rock, Christ Jesus, could restore and recreate such a beautiful fragrance of His goodness and grace again, as the scent of fresh rain. Little did the missionary ever understand the process and the plan by which God would create an enlarged capacity for the scent of rain and the essence of hope within him.

Had he known, he might have never said yes to Pastor John, and the scent of rain wouldn't have been smelt by so many resulting in new buds of purpose, passion, and life.

God Knows What He's About!

When God wants to drill a man, and thrill a man, and skill a
man, When God wants to mold a man to play the Noblest
part; When He yearns with all His heart, to create so great
and bold a man, that all the world shall be amazed, Watch
His methods, watch His ways! How He ruthlessly perfects,
whom He royally elects! How He hammers him and hurts
him, and with mighty blows converts him into trial shapes
of clay, which only God understands; While his tortured
heart is crying, and he lifts beseeching hands! How he
bends but never breaks, When His good he undertakes:

How He uses whom He chooses, and with every purpose
fuses him, by every act induces him, To try His splendor
out:

God knows what He's about. (Anonymous)

Cuts and wounds: An expectation minus (-) the present experience equals (=) disappointment, leaving one cut and wounded. Nighttime, nightmare entrance first night in the U.S.A., in the new "pastoral home," which the church arranged for their new pastor: the antithesis of "Home Sweet Home."

It was September 15th, 1999, and the missionary, along with his wife and four-year-old son, landed into Newark Liberty Int'l Airport—amidst of all things, a hurricane and RAIN, LOTS OF RAIN—as if the heavens had opened. Two members of the church had borrowed the church van to pick the missionary up. The ride home was dark. Heavy rain was pouring, and finally, the van pulled alongside a small home. Here they were, about to enter into a home they had never seen, but soon were to be paying for it out of their meager pastoral salary.

And the cuts began. Unmet expectations create cuts. A disappointment is the result of an appointment with an expectation that was never met.

First night—entrance into the U.S.A. The driver gets out of the vehicle and walks out into the pouring rain up to the house's front door—only to discover that he has not got the right key. He has keys, but NOT the right key for that door—an important door for the missionary's family. For the missionary, his wife and four-year-old son, the journey has been a 14-hour journey, and it's 3 a.m. (for the missionary as their bodies are on European time), and the driver returns to the van to remark, "We haven't the key. Somebody call Al."

Wonderful. Great way to begin a new chapter—stuck in a vehicle late at night, overly exhausted, and now having to wait for someone who has the key to drive over to unlock the door for the new pastor and his family! Finally, the key arrives and the missionary is ushered into the home, and in one swift instant, the previous expectations of a "pleasant home" are dashed to the ground as a crystal vase bursting into a thousand pieces for there before his eyes lies the interior of a home that is decrepit, outdated, crumbling and resembling a buffet of old yard sale furnishings. A complete contrast to the missionary's previous apartment, which was entirely remodeled with Macy's furnishings, with brand new sinks, faucets, flooring, draperies, etc. The missionary and his family had been fortunate enough to place on a container shipped to Romania the Macy's furnishings to make a home beautiful, fresh, and warm. But standing in front of them with the hurricane rain pouring down outside, was the interior to which the missionary's wife said, "Where did this junk come from?!"

The cut of disappointment only deepened as the missionary ran immediately across the street, knocked on the front door, which was opened by a stranger, Mary Jo. The missionary said, "Hello, I'm new here, just arrived and am moving across the street. Who in the world was living there?"

And the woman replied, "Oh, no one has lived there for years, it's been an abandoned house, for years, and before that, it was filled with several single adults. It's been known as a crack house."

Wow. Not the response the missionary had anticipated. Welcome to the first night in the U.S.A.

The cut deepened still as the days following would reveal that the house was rented, although with the pastor paying from his salary. The elder who had signed for the home had not even walked into the house to check it out before he signed the lease on behalf of the new pastor. Not such a good idea. That tactic wouldn't make the top 10 list of how to make your new pastor feel welcomed "home!"

The missionary would never forget that evening, watching his wife, although overly exhausted from the 14-hour trip crossing the Atlantic with a four-year-old child, waiting through customs, waiting in the rain for a key to the house, having to spend more than an hour that evening scrubbing the tub from the "filth" that she said remained.

After viewing the sofa, which resembled one from the 70s and smelt like you know what, the missionary's wife said, "I'm not sitting on that couch. Tomorrow you are going to have to throw that out, and we are going to have to get new furniture!"

The church people were asked to donate their old unwanted home furnishings so as their new pastor could begin life afresh and anew. So several did—their hearts were right—they did what they were asked to do, and some cleaned the best they knew. What they didn't know was that their pastor's wife was the

"Martha Stewart" of cleanliness and excellence. The missionary and his family entered their home in a hurricane. The thunder and lightning were soon to follow.

The Cut of a Balloon—The Piercing Pain of the Pop—Economical Cuts

A balloon mortgage popped, and rose 33%!!

Four days into his new pastorate at the young age of 32 in a church to which he had not sent his resume to nor asked to be their pastor, nor was seeking to be their pastor, nor had ever planned to be a pastor in the U.S.A, the vocabulary of this missionary-pastor expanded rather dramatically, upon learning from his secretary a new word. One which you don't want to learn this way.

Joni, the secretary, and financial booker replied to the pastor's question as to why the mortgage check was 33% more than the previous month's check. $3,700 more, in fact, raising the mortgage to $14,000. "Pastor, didn't they tell you?"

"Tell me what, Joni?"

"Didn't the elders tell you that there was a balloon mortgage?"

"Balloon mortgage, huh?" Now the mention of balloons used to cause the missionary's mind to think pleasant happy thoughts of parties and laughter, his four-year-old smiling while holding onto a balloon. But the word mortgage tied to a balloon—what is that? Sheepishly, the missionary pastor asked his secretary Joni, "What is a Balloon Mortgage?"

Joni replied, "Well, like all balloons, even the pretty ones, they all go POP! And like a balloon, the mortgage went POP—on September 19th—due to the schedule of the loan. I thought they would have told you."

The missionary's mind was about to POP. That was a little piece of information that they deemed not important to tell. The tree (the church) had been deeply cut that day economically as the balloon went POP!

The missionary discovered rather quickly the true measure of death—economically speaking—throughout the next several days. First, the church was more than $100,000 behind in account payables, including utilities. Second, the church wasn't able to pay its mortgage when it was $10,300 a month, so how they were going to pay for it now that it was $14,000, as was soon to be discovered—to the dismay of many.

Staff members who were being paid enormous salaries were soon to be requested to continue serving while receiving a compensation decrease—some

25%, some 50%, and some 75%, dependent on the priority of their service to the congregation. The missionary quickly learned that the call of God to serve was coupled together with economical commensuration, and within six months, approximately three staff members, along with 75 people, migrated to increase the attendance and immediate pleasure of other local churches! The missionary-pastor was learning how to expand and grow the "kingdom of God" through church migration—more so unintentional than intentional.

The church tree had been hacked down to the very stump. From the first week for the next 135 weeks—945 days—of the scorching, searing desert heat, unrelenting, piercing pain, and pressure were endured in the heart of the missionary pastor who felt responsible for keeping the big boat afloat financially while most of the crew and passengers were bailing quickly. It was a big boat, a 45,000 sq. Ft. of unfinished warehouse with a $1.25 million loan. When most everyone had written them off and the bank was literally signing a "death certificate" of acceleration of debt and repossessing the building, due to one word of God—a word of wisdom from Dr. Benjamin Crandall, former president of the Zion Bible Institute, now Northpoint Bible College— the missionary pastor began to smell the scent of rain. He hoped against all hope and purpose, passion, and life began to bud again. One word from God can change your life. One word from God believed causes the scent of rain to be smelt and for you to have hope again. New purpose, passion, and life will bud again.

Events transpired at the very 11:59th moment in which the church paid off their loan, received a refinancing from a bank following seven previous rejections, and secured, through wise and entrepreneurial out-of-the-box thinking, an $880,000 new tenant contract, resulting in, years later, raising the value of the property (purchased for $1.8 million) to a resale property value of $5 million. On March 11, 2008, they were 100% debt-free, with $3.35 million in the bank for a new beginning.

Though the tree was deeply cut, yet at the scent of rain, it will bud again. Undeniably, economically, the tree had bud again unto a new purpose, passion, and life.

I Have This Hope
by 10th Avenue North

As I walk this great unknown
Questions come, and questions go
Was there a purpose for the pain?
Did I cry these tears in vain?
I don't want to live in fear
I want to trust that You are near
Trust Your grace can be seen
In both triumph and tragedy
I have this hope
In the depth of my soul
In the flood or the fire
You're with me, and You won't let go
But sometimes my faith feels thin
Like the night will never end
Will You catch every tear?
Or will You just leave me here?
But I have this hope
In the depth of my soul
In the flood or the fire
You're with me, and You won't let go
So, whatever happens, I will not be afraid
Cause You are closer than this breath that I take
You calm the storm when I hear You call my name
I still believe that one day I'll see Your face
And I have this hope
In the depth of my soul
In the flood or the fire
You're with me
I have this hope
In the depth of my soul
In the flood or the fire
You're with me, and You won't let go.

CHAPTER 9

Four Seasons of Life—Where am I Now?

Where am I? What do I do now so I can smell the scent of rain to bud again? Throughout the next several pages, you will discover powerful practical truths for the seasons of your life, the principles and best practices within each season which, applied, will propel you into your next season successful and satisfied knowing that "You smell great!" For you're wearing the fragrance of the scent of rain (the perfume of petrichor) with you and into your next season/chapter.

Ecclesiastes expresses the cyclical view: "To everything, there is a season, and a time to every purpose under the heaven; a time to be born, and a time to die; a time to plant, and a time to pluck up that which is planted." As an optimist, it's easy for me to have read this verse and to focus on the seasons which I most enjoy: the time for new beginnings to be born—new ventures to plant—however, the realist must realize that God in His sovereignty knows the equal value which one can extract within the non-pleasurable seasons, the time "to die" and the time to "pluck up that which is planted."

Being a believer and having being immersed in the biblical passages of hope, faith, and love, it's not been easy for myself to come to grips with "a time to die," and plucking up that which is planted. For those who desire to be "mature," to have, through exercise of use and to be able to discern good from evil, then seasons which are uncomfortable, inconvenient, and downright disturbing must be perceived as 1) allowed by God, and 2) purposed by Him to mature us, whereby we become "sons and mature ones" not infants and toddlers in the faith.

First, let us explore the value of seasons—the many varied experiences, events, and epochs (length of time), which we all engage ourselves in at some point in time. The seasons of our lives are cyclical. Having grown up in Northern Maine, where potato farming was the main crop and large economic engine of the county, I understand seasons. When harvest time came to Aroostook County, everyone's life adjusted. The overflow of this new "season" affected the entire county. Schools were let out for 2-3 weeks, so kids as young as 12 could be hired to pick up the potatoes along the newly furrowed rows.

Cyclical concepts are patterns that are repeated but have different meanings at different times in our lives. They are not better or worse than earlier forms, merely different from them. We need to give ourselves often permission to experience life in a different form than our past-especially if we are to regain our purpose, passion, and life.

Our adult life can be experienced as a Ferris wheel or roller coaster, with ups and downs, times that are repeated over and over and over again in a cycle of continuity and change. We often experience periods of stability, followed by periods of transition. As adults, we adventure through both stable and unstable times, with many peaks and valleys, and have capacities for managing both. Our life is filled with long seasons of positive life chapters and troublesome life transitions.

As Henri Bergson wrote at the turn of the century: "To exist is to change; to change is to mature; to mature is to create oneself endlessly."

People who understand the seasons and times will DO the following:

1. Perceive life as an adaption to change: change within themselves and their environment.

2. Know how to seize new opportunities provided by change. Living with a season-cyclical view takes faith to trust and obey His word—even in the complete absence of any scent of rain along with a trust in the daily flow of His presence, that may not be felt. We must be willing to let go and to let God.

3. Recognize that life develops through cycles of change and continuity rather than in progressive, linear straight lines. This causes one to understand both what persists throughout our lives and what necessarily changes.

4. Honor both the ups and the downs of life, the blessings, and the curses. Conflicts and loss are part of everyday life, as are joy and ecstasy. Both are incorporated into the way we live and interact with one another.

5. Realize that our human systems are flexible, interactive, conflicting, and resilient, permitting continuous adaptions. They see all systems as cycles and interacting with each other. All systems have up and downtimes, and beginnings and endings. Adults learn to shape and adapt to these systems in different ways at different times and places, designing scenarios and making them happen and when they don't work disassembling them and creating new ones. There is no cultural master plan, no human prescription for fulfillment. As so, it can be said that faith is a journey and not a guilt trip!

6. Be aware that continuous learning is essential to the constant retooling of adult competence. We need not only knowledge and training to make our external world work but self-knowledge and training to make the inner world effective. It is far more challenging to learn how to "be" than to "do."

For so many, and for so long, much attention and intention has been to reshape and re-design our external worlds while neglecting the adjustments which were necessary for our internal worlds. Such neglect is revealed by those who may "move on" or enter into a new external season of life, have made a mini-transition externally, but internally they carry themselves into their new job. New home, new spouse, new church—yet the same dissatisfaction, disappointment, and dryness they had before. As per the adage: "Wherever you are, there You are." We must not neglect the nurturing of our soul.

There was an old song which they taught me years ago: "Jesus on the inside working on the outside. Oh, what a change in my life." From the inside out is where true transformation occurs. And yes, that is true—however, three decades later, I'm much more aware that His working on the inside is a full-time job, one which will last my lifetime.

Life is a roller coaster ride through changing seasons. Suddenly, turns jerk us this way and that, speeds pick up and slow down, we soar high and plunge low. As wild as the ride can be, life's seasons include the quiet times we find easier to negotiate, places where we regain orientation and retool for whatever is next. In every case, whatever the season, it is a period that is consequential, formative, and essential.

The transition between seasons is not always pleasant. That's the nature of the seasons. Over the long haul, the benefits become evident, but the upside is often difficult to see while the transition is underway. When the monarch butterfly lays her eggs, a series of transformation begins. The larvae feed on the leaf for approximately two weeks, by which time they become caterpillars. Soon, each caterpillar finds a twig and attaches itself head downward. In a matter of hours, the caterpillar sheds its skin and is transformed into a jade-colored chrysalis. In two weeks, the chrysalis releases the monarch butterfly, one of nature's most glorious creatures. The monarch's unmistakable beauty is developed over a series of unappealing seasons. Good times—not-so-good times.

In life, our mountaintop experiences are far more enjoyable, exciting, and more comfortable to embrace than our journeys to the valley. On our most difficult days, when everything in our season is seeming to work against us, finding our purpose in the valley can be like looking for a contact lens—one lost in the dark on your bedroom floor. It can be counterintuitive, at best. Nevertheless, the universal truth remains intact: to everything, there is a season and a time for every purpose under heaven. This cannot be denied.

Life seasons don't always fit together to us at the moment as a well-constructed Lego set. However, they are perfectly designed for us by the Designer of the Universe, who has our highest good within His heart for us. The constant shifting of our season discourages us from setting up camp beside stagnant waters. Yes, the Lord is our Shepherd: He will lead us beside the "still" waters, not the stagnant.

When we are aware, awake, and attentive to the purpose of the shifting of our seasons, we are positioned to see and seize our new vistas of opportunities.

No two seasons are identical. Each one requires us to regain a new perspective and a new response. Our takeaways in every season, whether good, bad, or indifferent, are that in EVERY season, there is a destiny, purpose, and new and positive possibilities for a brand new day! How much treasure you will be able to mine from your season has everything to do with the way you respond to it, whether you exercise appreciative inquiry: What's right about my season? What can I hold on to, let go of, take on, and move on?

Although in the wisdom of God, the predictability of the details of our soon-approaching new season are hidden from our view, our practical preparation can deepen our understanding into the purposes of God for the season, thus enabling us to either endure or enjoy all things, knowing that in everything, He makes all things beautiful and work together for His good. **Let's consider three principles that apply to all seasons.**

1. Each life season is unique in purpose and produces a "climate" conducive to personal growth and the achievement of that purpose, all in preparation for you to smell the rain.
2. Life's seasons will change regardless of our participation or cooperation with their purpose.
3. Life's past seasons are sealed in the annals of history. They cannot be changed, but they can continue to bear good fruit in the future.

When you can detect the onset of a new season and are open to the new conditions each season creates, you become fully present to the moment and position to gain from times of change. Your seasons, regardless of which season it is, become a place of power and purpose, a place where you are geared to make an impact. This is significant because taking ownership of your season hastens the fulfillment of your dreams.

When difficult seasons are behind us, it is easy to recognize just how destiny-connected they were. But this approach is "reactive, " and it keeps us playing catch up. When we respond from "behind" the curve, we miss the best destiny moments and opportunities encoded in each season. There is a much more productive approach, and that is to recognize each season and realize it's a vital connection to being a part of the petrichor process of the smell of rain, not as the season ends, but before it begins.

With every seasonal change in life, there are shifts in the weather, both externally (in your circumstances or relationships) and internally (in your feelings or your changing needs and desires). Becoming a good weather detector will help you to mine every morsel of destiny from each season because you experience shifts in each season.

If you become determined to take ownership of every season and deal with life's ups and downs positively, every circumstance will become an opportunity for victory. Every trial turned to a testimony. Every wound is a womb of a new beginning. Every scar turned to star, your setbacks to setups for the miraculous — tragedy to triumph. Every closed door unto an opened door—yes, different from what you had thought, but in the end, it will be better than you had ever imagined!

Every season gives you something to leverage. This includes seasons of ADVERSITY.

- Whether you have suffered a job loss, the death of a loved one, financial distress, or marital friction, you can find something positive to be gained from experience. A greater appreciation of every day lived, added wisdom in financial matters, increasing compassion for your mate—whatever it is, you can leverage your gains and improve your outcomes in future seasons.

- If you're in a season of crisis in your health, business, or family, you have an opportunity to discover your strengths and overcome your fears. As you weather the storm, you'll gain the self-confidence to handle subsequent crises with even greater confidence. Refining crises bring out the best in us; they develop our character and purify our motives.

Your ability to advance in every type of climate is dependent upon your willingness to focus on the positives in every season. If you are entering your most rewarding season (mountaintops) to date but are prone to attitudes of fault-finding, unforgiveness, ingratitude, or laziness, you will fail to enjoy the beauty of the season and you will undermine its outcome and may well possibly shorten your mountaintop season, cutting yourself off and swiftly sliding into a more tenuous season of the desert doldrums.

Conversely, if you are in the throes of a difficult season but are determined to maintain a positive outlook, then if you are gracious, forgiving, generous, thankful, and hopeful, your hard times will lead to unexpected triumphs, and yield favor with those who are called to be supportive of your destiny. When taking stock of the season you are in, remember that you are in a specific place and time for a reason. You are contending for your destiny! Avoid tunnel vision and refuse to view adverse circumstances with a magnifying glass. Instead, keep the big picture in view. Learn how to "see" what you do not yet have; as long as you can see your dream, you can move toward it.

In the midst of my most excruciating, peel-the-nail-back-off-my-finger pain, when I was feeling as if an ocean freighter had pinned me to the ocean floor, when my heart (mind, will, and emotions) felt as if all-purpose, passion, and life had been vacuum-sucked out of me, leaving a ghost of what I used to be, I enrolled as a student within the Hudson Institute of Santa Barbara CA. This decision determined not only the trajectory of my new life chapter and season, but it also left me for the first time in 25 years feeling "born again-again." As such, much of the principles and best practices from within this chapter were derived from the Hudson Institute, founded by Frederick Hudson. Upon completion of their nine-month Professional Coaching Certification program, I gained far more than a Professional Coaching Certificate; I gained a most invaluable friendship with a man named Bob Westenberg and transformative tools and teachings for purpose, passion, and life to bud again.

Key Question

- Where are you? Where are you really? At the Mountaintop of Peak Performance and Fulfillment?
- In the Wilderness/Desert of the Doldrums, with no wind in your sails?
- In the Valley of the "Shadow of Death:" the place of internal renewal and new creations are made in the dark.
- In the Plains of Planning: developing new skills, networking, and construction towards a dream.

Adults experience the cycle of change as a renewal cycle. As you proceed around the cycle, you will experience change as "growth" and development, renewal, evolving. The very movement around the circle keeps you on your learning edge. No place on the cycle is better or worse than anywhere else. Each has its time, place, and lesson.

Each place challenges us to extend ourselves as we move toward ever-increasing wholeness in experiencing *The Scent of Rain—Essence of Hope,* so new buds of purpose, passion, and life are revived within us, and in turn, we become as *The Scent of Rain—Essence of Hope* to others who so desperately need hope!

CHAPTER 10

Life 'Smelling the Scent of Rain' Skills

At least ten basic life skills represent the most important abilities (blessings and bridges) you need to grow and develop as a person, to succeed in each season, at creating life chapters, and at producing significant self-renewal during life transitions. These are human competencies that assume strategic importance at specific times in your life.

The ten skills are approximate notions. People require many other competencies for making their lives work, but these 10 are the generic human tasks in which adults today need basic proficiency for the weaving and unraveling of their lives to become an accomplished dream weaver, releasing the dream that was planted inside of each one us by the Master Gardener.

Although each skill has a time in the cycle of life when it performs a critical function, they are important at all times, because to some degree, parts of our lives are simultaneously at various places in the cycle. During a life chapter, there will be many times when minor transitions must be managed, and during transitions it is necessary to maintain a minimal life structure to take care of oneself. Each of the ten skills represents a strategic activity for a particular time and place in the cycle of life.

Four Seasons and Ten Life Skills

Each season is an experience of feelings of the inner self within the outer fields of ones' family, faith, friends, self, and work. One must recognize that one may be on the mountaintop in one area of life at yet in a valley within another field. Such is life.

1st Season: Mountaintop of Peak Performance and Fulfillment

- Wholly and fully alive to one's purpose.
- Enthusiastic with passion.
- Loving life. Loving others. Loving oneself.

In this season, plans are turned to action. Dreams are actualized. Hopes are realized. Big Hairy Audacious Goals are achieved. Balancing a checkbook is no problem; you rarely even look at the bank account balance. Your phone rings regularly with a constant flow of friends and new friends. Your confidence is strong as all the external indicators reveal that you are "on the top." Attendance is growing within the church, cash flow is no longer an issue, and the staff is sailing with the wind behind them. Your marriage is blossoming like a rose. The engine of work is running on all cylinders. There is a flow to your life.

You're vibrant, radiant. You're living a meaningful life. Yes, life can be better, but wow—you smell good today!

Life skills Required and Developed in This Season

1. Creative construction through imagining, visioning, showing the presence of your hopes and dreams.
2. Plateauing: Sabbath well. Resting and learning contentment with leaving a living legacy, fully satisfied. Plateauing well sustains and deepens a successful season/life chapter until its appointed end.

Second Season: Wilderness and Desert of Doldrums (No Wind in Your Sails)

To be commanded to love God at all, let alone in the wilderness, is like being commanded to be well when we are sick, to sing for joy when we are dying for thirst, to run when our legs are broken. But this is the first and great commandment, nonetheless. Even in the Wilderness, especially in the wilderness—you shall love Him! (Frederick Buechner)

Herein is the season in which it feels literally as though there is "no air in one's sail." Life is quickly losing its meaning. The tree which once was blooming and producing bountiful fruit has been cut. Suddenly or slowly, the pain is the same. Life feels to be flowing out and away from oneself. Many common triggers can thrust one out of a mountaintop season and experience into the Wilderness, or Desert, whether one has been led into such a wilderness as Jesus Christ was, or one was "forced by external factors" as Ruth and Isaac and Joseph. The experience of pain, perplexities, pressure, fear, and bewilderment are the same.

Experiences and voices that shout out into one's soul and spurt the words "Cancer," "You're fired," "I don't love you nor want you anymore," "It's over," "It's all your fault," "You're a failure," have drowned out the once-clear resounding sound and song of faith, and today you feel as if you've reached a dead end. Life will never be the same as it was again. Hope seems to be lost entirely, at least for you. In the Wilderness and Desert of Doldrums, one feels the loss of energy, confidence, and willpower because one has lost their vision and vitality. When in the Doldrums, it's not long after one loses their "want to" that they quickly lose their "how-to" and then their "why," causing them to succumb to hopelessness. When our Why is greater than our How, we will always find a way out.

As we are goal-oriented creatures, hope is inextricably linked to achievement, and when a sense of vision departs, willpower follows shortly after that, and this invariably affects our mood and outlook. Within the Doldrums, one feels stuck, often seized by the paralysis of analysis. The Bible states that hope deferred makes the heart sick, but when the desire comes, it is the Tree of Life. Within the wilderness and Desert, one often is exasperated with the depths of the divide between one's expectations and one's experience. The great gap is filled at the onset with negative energy, which draws one away, down a current of cynicism, criticalness, and constant negative thinking, which only reinforces the current downward cycle. It is possible, however, that one can transform the negative energy into positive energy-to reverse the reversals, to press past that which is felt, seen by one's natural senses to enter into the unseen realm, to hear and see the future as it is calling and yet coming into existence. How?

When you find yourself here in the Wilderness and Desert of Doldrums, it's hardest to smell the scent of rain and hope again with a full sense of purpose, passion, and life. Yet were one to act by faith and do the practical 4 Steps to smell the scent of rain, one's purpose, passion, and life would bud again, as discovered in the next chapter (Chapter 11).

In the natural, climatic process of the production of the scent of rain, it is in the driest drought, hottest arid areas and seasons in which the most fragrant scent of rain is produced. As in the natural, so in the spiritual. We are aware that there are no diamonds without enormous pressure and high heat. We hear that the cream always rises to the top. We recognize that the stars that shine the brightest shine in the darkest of night. And yet even for the soul to shine, for life to truly live, there requires the fires of affliction. Our perception of our Wilderness and Desert season prohibits or prepares one from smelling the rain.

Remember Job? Consider his perception. Perceptions position one for connection. Connection creates clarity. Clarity creates power. Power to be and power to do. Consider Job and perception of his wilderness, the desert season in which He was deeply cut like a tree.

Look, I go forward, but He is not there, and backward, but I
cannot perceive Him; when He works on the left hand, I
cannot behold Him; when He turns to the right hand, I
cannot see Him. But He knows the way that I take; when He
has tested, me, I shall come forth as gold. (Job 23:8-10)

What a classic description of the wilderness. Job searched for the presence and moving of God in his life. Yet the more he searches, the more elusive God seems. God, however, is working on Job's behalf and knows exactly what is happening in Job's life. So just because God's presence is not readily noticeable, it does not mean He is not there and working in our lives.

My friend, you have to believe, and please rehearse this phrase until it soaks down into the very roots of your being. **God is working right now, changing things, realigning events, adjusting circumstances, and influencing people to meet my needs.** When you first received the Lord Jesus and filled with the Holy Spirit, God's presence was wonderfully real to you. You would call His name, and instantly He responded. When you prayed, He manifested His presence. As a newborn child in His family, you received the attention given to a baby. When children are newly born, they require constant care. They must be fed, clothed, and bathed, and they rely on others to do everything for them. However, as children grow, they must be allowed to mature. When our youngest daughter began to feed herself, she became frustrated because she couldn't put her food in her mouth as quickly or efficiently as her mommy. Now she struggled to receive what once had come so easily. Many times it would have been easier for all of us if we had continued feeding her, instead of allowing her to do it for herself. However, if we had taken the "easy" way, her maturing in this area would have been significantly hindered. As babies grow, the level of assistance they receive changes to encourage growth and development.

God does this with us so we can develop and mature spiritually. When we are newly born again and filled with His Spirit, for a season, He manifests Himself at our every cry. To foster maturity, He allows us to go through times in which He does not respond instantly to our every call. The time comes when a character must be developed. Romans 5:2-5: "And we rejoice in the hope of the Glory of God. Not only so, but we also rejoice in our sufferings because we know that suffering perseverance, perseverance, character, and character, hope. And hope does not disappoint us, because God has poured out his love into our hearts, by the Holy Spirit, whom he has given us..."

And when tribulation refuses to let up, the character begins to rise. When the character begins to rise, hope begins to show up. When hope begins to show up, disappointment can no longer speak up. When disappointment no longer speaks up, vision begins to show up! And the Wilderness and the Desert are where it is done. "...the wilderness where God appears to be miles away and His promises even farther. He is, however, close at hand, for He has promised never to leave nor forsake us" (Hebrews 13:5).

It is a time when you appear to be going in the opposite direction from your dreams and the promises He made you. You perceive no growth and development. In fact, you may feel you are regressing. His presence seems to diminish rather than grow. You may feel unloved and even ignored. But you are not. Maturity of character is developed in us by God when we are in the Wilderness. The Wilderness is where the fruit of the Spirit is cultivated. The Wilderness is a dry place. It may be dry spiritually, financially, socially, or physically. It is here that God gives 'daily" bread, not "abundance of things." He meets our needs at this time, not necessarily our wants. The purpose of the wilderness is to purify us, to prepare us to the fresh smell of rain on and in our dry souls.

Our pursuit is to be His heart, not his provision. Then, when we come into sufficient times, we won't forget that it was the Lord our God who gave us abundantly to establish His covenant (Deuteronomy 8:2018).

The Wilderness is a Time of Testing: "The Lord your God led you...in the wilderness, to humble you and to test you, to know what was in your heart" (Deuteronomy 8:2).

The Wilderness is the location of God's highway. It is in the Wilderness that the way is prepared for you to make a successful mini-life transition or to create a brand new life chapter. To change or make the transition, we must be willing to leave the comfortable, secure, and familiar. As we have seen, the wilderness is the place where God tests us, humbles us, refines us, and works His character in us. It is the preparation ground for one's purpose, passion, and life to bud again. The most exciting thing about the wilderness is that it is the place where God reveals Himself in a fresh new way!

Notice again what Isaiah 51:3 says: "For the Lord shall comfort Zion; He will comfort all her waste places, and He will make her wilderness like Eden, and her desert like the garden of the Lord, joy, and gladness shall be found therein thanksgiving, and the voice of melody."

Where was Moses when God revealed himself to him in the burning bush? In the wilderness (Exodus 3:1-4).

Where was John the Baptist when God revealed himself to John? In the wilderness (Luke 3:2-3).

Where was Paul when God revealed Himself to Paul and called him to preach among the heathen? In the wilderness (Galatians 1:16-17).

Where was John the apostle when he received The Revelation of Jesus Christ? A wilderness, a deserted island called Patmos. (Revelation 1:9)

Where was Joseph when God revealed Himself so Joseph could interpret the dreams of the baker and the butler and eventually Pharaoh? A Prison of Wilderness.

Where was God when God revealed Himself to David as his "Shepherd, His strength, his shield, and His fortress, in the wilderness of rejection of his Father-in-Law King Saul, Betrayal of his son and companions."

It is in the wilderness that the Lord revealed Himself to us in a fresh way. Isaiah 45:15 says: "Verily, thou art a God that hideth himself, O God of Israel, the

Savior. The Lord hides Himself to those who are not hungry for Him, but to those who seek and search for Him with all their hearts, he will reveal Himself to them."

Many give up in the desert—in their dryness and dearth—but God is saying, "keep pressing onward, don't stop!" We must have a persistent and tenacious drive within us that won't stop until His will is done

Life Skills in the Wilderness

1. Deconstruction-eliminating of the old to prepare for the new.

   Letting go to let come. Coming to terms with a decline, negative emotions, and feeling trapped in an increasingly dysfunctional life chapter.

2. Listening, hearing and perceiving the Voice of God and our authentic voice.

   It has been said that the real voyage of discovery consists not in seeing new landscapes, but in having fresh eyes. Perception determines the reception of positive or negative energy resulting in an "I can or an I can't" mentality.

Third Season: The Valley of the Shadow of Death: Where Inner Renewal and New Creations are made in the Dark!

In pursuit of your life's purpose, there will inevitably occur a life-changing crisis in the form of a refining fire setting you free from a confining limitation, thus empowering you unto greatness.

- In the Valley, we do our cocooning of the inner self-transformation from the inside out.
- In the Valley, we begin to experience a restoring of our soul. A re-emergence of our authentic self.

Is God silent unto you? Are you in a Season of Deafening Silence?

Giving up is not an option.

Have you ever wondered how a caterpillar becomes a beautiful butterfly? Many caterpillars use the silk of the cocoon to fasten themselves to a plant. Inside the cocoon, the metamorphosis takes place. Now here's the incredible part: When the metamorphosis is complete, the butterfly, despite wet and limp wings, struggles to pull itself out of the cocoon, spreads its wings, and then hardens them by forcefully pumping blood into them. When the wings are stiff, the butterfly pumps the blood back out of its wing veins, and it's ready to take flight.

But do you know what happens to a butterfly if some unsuspecting, well-intentioned passerby sees it struggling and helps it out of its cocoon? It dies. Why? Because the butterfly's efforts to leave the cocoon and prepare its wings are what give it the strength it needs to fly. Without the fight, its wings won't be sturdy enough to support itself. The butterfly must struggle to be strong and beautiful. And so must you and I. We are to fight the good fight of faith.

How many times have you wanted to give up on your dream of becoming a brilliant teacher?

Don't give up. Embrace the metamorphosis you're experiencing. While you're in the cocoon, examine your inside world by shedding the old skin of self-limiting belief systems, incongruent behavior patterns, and sabotaging language that negates your destiny. When you understand that your transformation process is an inside job, you'll gladly embrace every trial, challenge, problem, and issue as an opportunity to grow.

Break free from the things that are holding you back. Release the need to fight the struggles and learn to accept them. Celebrate the challenges, for it is only through struggle that you can emerge from the cocoon, a strong, beautiful butterfly. It's time to soar and release your brilliance!

Life Skills in the Valley of the Shadow of Death: A Cocooning, Self-Renewal Phase

1. Ending well. Designing your funeral before your real funeral. Ending a life chapter with dignity and care requires an ability to say farewell with gratitude and clarity, leaving you free to consider your options.
2. Cocooning. Cocooning clearly and successfully by sorting things out results in a personal plan. What to keep, what to eliminate or change, what to add, and how to proceed into a revitalized life chapter. Cocooning is the first activity of a life transition turning inward to take stock, to find your basic values, and to disengage emotionally and mentally from the life chapter. If the life chapter cannot be redeemed, or if the optimal choice is to leave it to find a new and different one, the first step is to wholly live into a life transition where this skill is required. A life transition is like major surgery, usually resulting in personal development, new life options, and even transformation.

3. Renewing one's soul. Reflecting well. Journaling regularly. Discovering a new song, a new melody, and a new voice for your next season. Self-renewal follows from successful cocooning. It is the ability to be self-sustaining, producing confidence, energy, purpose, and hope. Self-renewal also involves a reevaluation of core issues and beliefs.

Fourth Season: The Plains-Planning Stage

In this season, new buds are arising in the natural. Fresh buds of grass are evident on the lawn of your life. You're on the road to your comeback. You're well on your way towards your preferred future with a clear new voice trained through your wilderness and valley season. Your song has a new harmony as you stitch together notes and lyrics into a melody of testimony for successfully passing through your valley. You're about to ascend again, bud again up onto another mountaintop. Here your creativity begins to be unleashed with enthusiasm. When you awake in the morning, your mind is already planning the day before you sip the first cup of coffee. You've been dreaming and planning, even in your sleep. You've gained new strength in a renewed sense of purpose. Feeling alive and playful, you begin to link up with new social support and new information about life options. Your renewed, revived self now feels anchored and purposive again, so you intentionally spend time exploring new external possibilities for a better life. Sooner or later, a new and compelling dream begins to take over with clarity as to how to develop your new dream, how to graze again upon the new field of possibilities.

Life Skills Required in This Season

1. Planning: A plan schedules the goal, a dream with available resources and possibilities. A goal is a dream with a deadline. Better to have a goal than no goal at all. Better to aim at the moon and hit the telephone phone than to never get off the pavement at all. Goals are to be SMART goals. Specific (what is to be done?) Measurable (how will you know it meets expectations?) Achievable (can the person do it?) Relevant (should it be done and why?) and Timely (when will it be done?)

2. Experimenting: Giving oneself permission to be creative, learning, exploring, risk-taking, and networking. When one is ready to venture back into a life chapter to venture into a new initiative, a new

relationship, a new social or spiritual environment, one takes on this skill.

3. Launching: There is no turning back. You've decided to move forward. This requires personal commitment, perseverance, adaptations, social, and economic alignment congruent to your goals.

We must be reminded that God moves in cycles and seasons and that we must learn to master the art of moving with Him in the cycles of life. This is our Divine Dance with Destiny.

We may find ourselves in seasons in which everything works well, and we achieve our goals, and then subsequently, when we plateau, we can very easily reach the conclusion that our tree has been cut. We may have received a word that God is shutting one door behind us and opening another ahead of us: we may not, however, realize that between the shutting of one door and the opening of another, is a long dark corridor, perhaps even a journey throughout the Wilderness and the Valleys of life before we return into a Plains season of positive planning of our preferred future again. When in the dark corridor, the Wilderness and Valley seasons/environments, it can often appear that there is no way back to our previous season/experience and no apparent way forward to the future—that is what we call being "stuck" within the Doldrums of life. However, this season often offers the greatest dividends available unto an individual who is willing to endure hardness and to continue living by faith and not by sight. It is the opportunity to reinvent oneself and thus reinvent one's future.

Each life skill leverages you through a particular portion of the cycle of change and prepares you for the next leg of the journey. Knowing which competencies to favor at various points of your cycle is the wisdom of one's life.

I Can Hear Naomi Sing the Song of Storyteller
by Morgan Harper Nichols

Oh the mountain where I've climbed
The valley where I fell
You were there all along
That's the story I'll tell
You brought the pieces together
Made me this storyteller
Now I know it is well, it is well

That's the story I'll tell
You hold the broken
You hear my every cry, every cry
My eyes are open
I know that it is well; it is well.

CHAPTER 11

The Four-Step Process That Increases Your Ability to Smell-the Scent of Rain: Essence of Hope.

- So my purpose, passion, and life will bud again. This bud is for you!
- So I experience a comeback with payback!
- So I learn how to turn my devastation into dividends of compensation and restoration!

Within the scriptures, there lies a tiny book of only four chapters, which is sandwiched between the book of Judges and Samuel, a book named Ruth. Although Ruth remains the centerpiece of the book, the scent of rain was the first smelt by Naomi, her mother-in-law.

Naomi experienced the scent of rain through the practice of this four-step process, resulting in her buds of purpose, passion, and life reviving again in ways that were abundantly above all that she could ever ask or think.

Naomi had once been, as many Israelite women, happily married to a respectable man of means. She had two young boys. She lived within a desirable suburb of Bethlehem, which means House of Bread, and enjoyed the goodness of life with little lack and suffering. Naomi's name means Pleasant-Desirable. Her life was indeed pleasant; she was living the "Desirable" life. It's not a stretch to consider that she also was the subject of morning gossip and evening's envy during neighborhood ladies' tea and nightcaps. And then her husband came home one day and said: "Naomi-get packing, we're moving to Moab." The carpet was pulled out from under her feet within one day. Times had been changing in Bethlehem for some time. The town once known for having an economic surplus, high employment, social amenities and services for its citizens, had slipped steadily into an economic slump, while inflation and unemployment had risen like a raging flood and worst of all, in the grocery stores it was clearly evident things had gotten from bad to worse—there was no bread on the shelves...empty bread shelves. Naomi had thought that they, of all people, might have been able to weather this famine, for it had not rained in such a long time, the crops had wilted and wasted away with no harvest, resulting in empty bread shelves.

Crisis, chaotic currents of change and furious fists of trouble pounded incessantly and immediately upon Naomi's door that day. She went from living in a Mountaintop Peak Performance season unto a torrid tumbling downward descent of a Wilderness/Desert season and continued into a Valley Season, which precipitated a most serendipitous and fortuitous events resulting in a powerful petrichor experience wherein she would smell the scent of rain and regain, reclaim and restore her purpose, passion, and life again!

Fast forward with me to the end of Chapter 4 and therein read a incredible account of Naomi, within her home seated in a rocking chair holding a grandson who was a "miracle baby," who would one day, beyond all odds, become the grandfather of the King of Israel. Obed was his name, and David, King of Israel, was his grandson!

Naomi's experience within the destructive, debilitating, denigrating Wilderness/Desert stripped her of her sense of security and identity, in such a deep, penetrating way that she actually changed her name from Naomi which meant "Pleasant and Desirable" into "Mara," meaning "Bitterness." She saw no practical, purposive pleasantness in her path of life, yet within her heart lay the dormant seeds of HOPE, the intrinsic invisible components capable of creating the smell of rain. The dormant seeds, although dormant, were not dead. The searing, burning loss from the death of her husband while she was living in a foreign country among strangers of a foreign culture, and religion, could not kill the dormant seeds of hope and life within her. The even more scathing, peel-back-your-fingernail pain she had experienced as she buried not one but two of her only children, her sons, could not and did not destroy and wipe out completely the ember, the seed of hope and life within her. Oh, how strong the seed of hope is!

And thus one day, while living in Moab as a widow, motherless, alone, seemingly forgotten, impoverished in her identity, emasculated emotionally, and wiped out economically, her dreams dashed, life had left her a wilted, worn, weary, wasted form of what she once was and within her mouth was the taste not of the "sweet life" but of "bitterness," and on that day and in that moment, out of the blue, blew a fragrance that filled her nauseated nostrils with that all but forgotten feeling and fragrance: HOPE. The scent of rain and the essence of hope had returned! God had revisited Bethlehem with rain! Literally the famine had finished its course, and Bethlehem, the House of Bread, once again had bread returning to its grocery shelves! It was upon hearing this good news, Naomi was able to smell the scent of rain.

And thus, the moment Naomi began to smell the scent of rain, she began to demonstrate the Four Steps to smell the rain skillfully so, in her purpose, passion, and life, she would regain, reclaim and sustain!

Here are the Four Steps to Smell the Scent of Rain

Step 1: Hold On (Celebrate What is Right with You and Around You)

Hold on to a promise: His promises, His word, His seed of truth, however tiny—even as tiny as a mustard seed. Hold it and acknowledge it, even amidst the doubt, the despair, the unbelief, hold it. Can one still have faith and doubt or despair and even a destructive identity language that exists at the same time? Yes, for some that may be a hard pill to swallow. Swallow it. You, despite what they may tell you, and what you tell yourself, you are NOT ALL THAT! And it's okay; I permit you to feel, to be real and reveal that you do have fears that co-mingle with your faith, that you do feelings of hope and feelings of hopelessness all within the same hour, that you do have emotions of joy and jarrings of deep sadness.

Give yourself the gift of permission to be...whatever you are at the moment, to be and then to choose your response, and when that response is reciprocal with the scent of rain steps and petrichor process, then it's not an "if you will smell the rain" but "When you will smell the rain" and "how strong will the scent of the rain be." Your choices within your everyday life can increase or decrease the strength of the scent of the smell of rain. Hold onto the confession of your faith, for He is faithful who has promised....

"Hold on" in the Greek comes from the word *katecho,* meaning to grip tightly as a wrestler will grasp onto an opponent and hold on to the mat with all their weight. Literally, "throw all your weight, however small it may seem to be" onto the "seed of your promise"—His word. Lean into the wind, lean on Him when you're not strong, and He'll be your friend, He'll help you carry on. Sometimes in our lives, we all have pain, we all have sorrow, but if we are wise, we know that there's always tomorrow. Lean on Him.

The old song which was taught to me in Mars Hill Full Gospel Church was: "I'm learning to lean, I'm learning to lean, I'm learning to lean on Jesus, I'm finding more power, every day and every hour, I'm learning to lean on Jesus."

Lean-shift your weight, your attention, and intention onto that seed and hold on...with all your might, and even when you feel that you've come to the end of your strength, know what you've just touched is the beginning of His. He will never, never, ever let you go.

I first learned to "lean-to shift my weight to another side" and totally trust the words of my father, on a sunny afternoon in the mountains of Vermont. My dad had taken me four-wheeling—not on these modern-day four-wheelers...but in his land rover. Dad loved to go four-wheeling. I could never understand it at first; however, the experience was thrilling and exciting... Dad loved to go, "off-road." He thrived on the "off-road" experience. He wasn't afraid. Dad would turn off the beaten paved road, and drive right into the woods, rolling over bushes, riding over deadened tree stumps, climbing over raised rocks. It seemed like the more dangerous the ascent was, the more he thrived. And that day was a day that I learned to "shift my weight" and lean into the "other side" to survive.

We have climbed a steep mountainside up onto the summit, viewed the breathtaking panoramic vista before us, and breath in and cool crisp, refreshing mountain air. Having gone up, we must then go down. And as all-mountain climbers know, the descent down a mountain is more dangerous than the ascent. More mountain climbers die descending a mountain than climbing up a mountain.

That day, for some reason, Dad chose to avoid descending through the growth of trees, rocks, and stumps and chose to descend along the cleared-out path of the edge of the ravine, which had a sheer drop of more than a hundred feet onto the rocky ravine floor. The path downward, although clearer of brush, trees, and rocks, was narrower and left little room of error for the driver lest the land rover slips off the edge of the ledge, crashing down into the ravine, resulting in certain death for us all.

We were coming very close to the edge of the ledge that day, and sitting on the right side of the back seat as Dad very slowly, cautiously drove along on edge, I could see down into the ravine. It was deep, and I was terrified of heights.

We heard it first—the slipping of the passengers' rear wheel in the dirt and off the rocks, over the edge, and simultaneously. Dad's voice was yelling, "Everyone lean LEFT, lean left, towards the far left side of the vehicle!" As we all, three or four of us, immediately dove and leaned our bodies against the left side of the windows in the back, you could feel the land rover tip and raise several inches, leaving the right front and back wheels off the ground, allowing Dad to steer the left tires further onto the path whereupon the path widened and upon so, Dad's voice yelled out again: "It's okay, you can shift your weight, all four tires are on the ground, and we're safe." Wow. Hold on. Shift all your weight even with your fears for they are real, onto the "other side" that one word which you've received from God, the one promise that you're holding onto and wait. However long, however hard and in time, your wheels will settle upon the ground. You will get your feet back on the ground-you will smell the rain again.

What else can we hold onto in the moments where we feel all is lost, and hope is gone?

Hold onto what is right in your life, even if you have to look deeper. Examine what is "right within your life," so you can celebrate what is right. Hold on to that which has been and is good. Hold on to truth, and it's true if you choose to believe it. Believe that God is good. Believe that God has a purpose for your life. Believe that God's thoughts for you are thoughts of good to give you a future and a bright hope. (Jeremiah 29:11) Believe that amidst all the destruction, devastation, and deprivation that you are experiencing, there is something, someone to celebrate. Praise God for the possibilities that do exist, and you'll discover more, and begin to smell the scent of rain.

Excerpt Material from Dewitt Jones: Celebrate What's Right with the World

Do we choose to see those possibilities? Do we truly believe that they're there? Perception controls our reality, and if we don't believe it, we won't see it. Dewitt Jones recounts a story that underscores this point.

I remember one time they sent me out to the Selkirk Mountains of British Columbia. I came upon this great field of dandelions. But I just wasn't into it, and I started to say, "Well, the light isn't right, I'll come back tomorrow." We've all been there. It happens all the time. At home, at work. "I just can't get into it. I'll do it tomorrow." And then tomorrow turns into next week and by the time I got back there ... no more dandelions. I had puffballs. That wasn't the way I had planned it."

And I was just about to leave when a little voice inside me said, "Come on, Dewitt, what's here to celebrate? I know it wasn't how you planned it, but what's right with the situation? Where are the possibilities?"

Before I knew it, I was into puffballs. Puffballs, puffballs! Over the puffballs, at eye level with the puffballs, under the puffballs, looking at them from every angle until ...

WOW, that's what I found. It was there. It seemed it was always there... if I was open enough to see it.

The more I shot for the Geographic, the more I realized what a powerful force our vision could be. As I celebrated what was right with the world, I began to build a vision of possibility, not scarcity. Possibility, always another right answer...

A vision that showed me that no matter how bleak and desolate, no matter how dry and devoid of possibilities the situation might seem, that if I was open to it... I could always find a perspective. In this case, just by dropping down in that crack in the slick rock and looking back. A perspective that would transform the ordinary...into the extraordinary.

As Michelangelo once wrote, "I saw an angel in the stone and carved to set it free."

Hold on to the promises He has given you. Hold on to the possibilities right around you. He is setting you free, opening unto you a new door of opportunity to a better life.

Hold on to His everlasting hand, for He is holding you. The old song said it well, "I'm gonna Hold, I'm gonna Hold, to God's unchanging hand. I'm gonna Hold, I'm gonna Hold to the one who understands, when my burden gets heavy, and I feel so sad, Jesus comes along and makes me feel so glad. I'm gonna hold, I'm gonna hold to God's unchanging hand. Hold on to Him—He's holding on to you."

Step 2: Let Go and Let God (Mute the Volume of the Negative Voices in the Head)

Perhaps the most important step we can take is to let go of emotional wounds. If one desires to smell the scent of rain and experience an increase in sensing more of God's presence, purpose, and passion within one's life, one must learn to "let go." We've all seen people who use their past emotional wounds as an excuse for making poor choices today. It doesn't work for them, and it won't work for you and I. We can't keep blaming our past for our present circumstances or the basis of our bad attitude or a rationalization for our unwillingness to forgive someone. The past is past, and it has NO power over our present and future unless we permit it. It's time to allow the fresh rain of His presence, purpose, and passion for healing your emotional wounds, it's time to let go of excuses and stop feeling sorry for yourself. It's time to get rid of the victim mentality.

The old song said it best: "He never promised there'd only been sunshine, He never said there would be no rain, He only promised a heart full of singing at the very things that once brought pain." Give them all. Give them. Give them all to Jesus, and He will turn your sorrows into joy. Quit comparing your life to somebody else's and quit dwelling on what could have been, should have been, or might have been. Quit asking questions such as Why this? Or why that, or why me?

We must learn to take our broken eggs and turn them into scrambled eggs, to take what God has permitted and make the most of it.

God allows by His wisdom that He could have prevented by His power to come into your life. You may have suffered very much, experiencing great and terrible hardships, or been through a lot of negative things. The deep scars that remain from you being lacerated are real reminders of the injustice you have suffered, but don't let your past determine your future. You can't do anything about what's happened to you, but you can choose how you will face what's in front of you. Holding onto feelings of bitterness and resentment will only poison your future. Let go of those hurts and pains. Forgive the people who did you wrong and, most importantly, forgive yourself for the mistakes you've made.

Some even need to forgive God. Perhaps you've been blaming God for taking one of your loved ones. Maybe you are angry at God because He didn't answer your prayers, or some situations didn't work out the way you had hoped. Regardless, you will never smell the scent of rain and experience His strong sweet scent of presence, purpose, and passion, as long as you harbor bitterness in your heart. You will wallow in self-pity, always feeling sorry for yourself, thinking that life hasn't dealt you a fair hand, as you thought you should have received. It's time to let go by changing the channel of your attention and intention. Letting go doesn't dissolve or cause the pain or fear to disappear immediately, nor does it absolve the offender of their responsibility to do justice and make amends, but slowly and surely as one redirects their focus—what they are paying attention unto—like changing the channel on the radio or turning the "antennae" from one direction another in order to receive a better "connection," we must let go, and turn our attention onto what we do have: His promises, present possibilities, and a permanent purpose! As we take celebrate what is right about our life and around our life, ever slowly, those feelings of fear will slip away, and the throbbing searing pain will subside.

Litany Against Fear by Frank Herbert

I must not fear. Fear is the mind-killer. Fear is a little-death that brings total obliteration. I will face my fear. I will permit it to pass over me and through me and when it has gone past I

will turn the inner eye to see its path. Where the fear has gone
there will be nothing. Only I will remain.

Yes, you will remain because you've learned how to smell the scent of rain. Naomi needed to let go, and let God in, to strongly smell the rain.

For her, as for many of us, letting go was a process. I propose unto you that she took one step, one day at a time within this process as often you and I. We understand that she was willing to let go of her past by the fact that she decided one day to pack her belongings and prepare to have one last meal with her two daughters-in-law. She even discouraged her daughters-in-law from traveling with her, although they expressed the desire to do so. Her smell of the scent of rain was only strong enough to hold hope for herself. She couldn't see how there was enough of the rain for her daughters-in-law. So she said, "I can't promise you anything, where I am going, but I'm returning unto Bethlehem. I need to go back home, for word has traveled that indeed God has answered prayer and rained upon the dry, barren land, whereas vegetation is returning, fields are sprouting, new life is budding, there is hope, and I'm headed home." So she let go—of the only close family she had, however painful it was and began the long walk home.

However, we see that the process of letting go does take time, and your life, as well as mine, reflects the same. One should not be bound by guilt, paralyzed by feelings of condemnation simply because one is aware that we today are "not measuring up." We are still lightly holding onto things we thought we let go of: yet have not completely. We must still move forward, one step at a time. And so Naomi, even as she crosses into the border of Israel, even as she approaches the city limits of Bethlehem, has not completely discarded the garment of guilt and shame—her identity has been emaciated, emasculated and decimated by the devastation and pain she has experienced. She doesn't see or feel desirable or pleasant on the inside, and thus, when neighbors who had known her years earlier turn closer to peer at this "stranger" coming into town, they remark in both disbelief and cloaked joy "Naomi! Is it you?!"

Out of her mouth come the words which reflect her internal belief system that simply won't let go, or hasn't been let go. Naomi replies: "No, it isn't. Don't call me Naomi; call me Mara because my life is nothing at all pleasant or desirable. Call me Mara, for bitterness has come upon me, and the only taste in my mouth right now is the bitter taste of disappointment, unmet expectations, anger towards my dead husband, grief over the loss of my two sons, shattered dreams and broken hopes. Call me Mara."

Now before we judge Naomi, let us open our heart towards her with grace. Observe the good. She has taken the step of holding onto what was right and true, the promises of God and the possibilities with her and in front of her, and had stepped further to let go of her present geographical location, her daughters-in-law, stepped towards Israel, letting go as best as she could of her fears, frustration and perceived failures, one step at a time, until she has finally arrived in Bethlehem, and we see there is more work to be done for her to experience an identity makeover—to be rebranded from the inside-out—she must smell stronger and inhale deeper the scent of rain, and so she continues to inhale by taking the next step.

Step 3: "Take ON" (Identity: Take on a New One)

She has transitioned from one season unto another, leaving Moab was as the larvae pushing and climbing out of the cocoon to be transformed into a butterfly. She was stepping into the season of "the Planning State" or what I'd call the "Plains"—the season of planting and cultivating the fields in the hope of the harvest.

Often, during this season of the Planning Stage or Taking On, we realize that because we have let go of something or someone or someplace, we have created either consciously or subconsciously "open space" for the new to be birthed, to break through the crust of the earth, and for the "bud" of new life to be seen! It's as one is actually co-laboring with the universe in co-creating the future, which is waiting to be born—to arrive. And by letting go, we can now "let come" the future as it seeks to appear.

Like so many others in this season, Naomi takes on a new role in her life: she is now the mentor, the guide, the teacher unto Ruth, her daughter-in-law. Despite the pleas of Naomi for Ruth to return unto her homeland, religion, customs, and culture, Ruth refused to turn back and responded with the all-too-favorite, well-known verse: "Your people will be my people, and your God will be my God."

And so, Naomi took on the role of guiding, instructing, mentoring Ruth in the customs, cultures, and community values of Israel—all of which caused Naomi to reflect upon the familiar, the known, and that which she had for so many years had believed. She as a result of taking on a new role was "sharpening her own saw" she was replenishing, refurbishing, retooling, renewing her spirit and life with the truth had been taught unto her as a little child, and in so doing, the scent of rain was going stronger and stronger unto her. Hope was rising, doubts and fear were fading. There indeed was hope for a tree, though she had been cut, lacerated so deeply and painfully. At the scent of rain, she would regain, reclaim purpose, passion, and life again.

She was discovering purpose in mentoring, "mothering" another, protecting and sheltering one as a mother eagle her young. For now, the tables had turned. Ruth was now the "stranger living in a strange land," dependent upon Naomi for instruction, guidance, and support.

Now, what about you? What possibilities are present around you right now for taking on new assignments, new skills, new roles, new relationships? Now that you have created open space within your life and mind by letting go—and by moving on, you do have open space, a vacuum if you will, that will be filled either intentionally or unintentionally. Perhaps some interests have been hidden deep beneath the surface of your soul, desires, dreams, that have been dormant. Today, write them down on a piece of paper. Create a list of new places, new faces, new steps, and new skills, which you would most like to "take on" into your newly desired, created future. God desires to co-create the future with you, for you are a co-laborer with God. Allow him to "carve-out from within you," the angel within. Go ahead, take the risk. You'll definitely miss 100% of the shots you never take! You have permission to experiment with new life. It's yours, so live it, truly live it. As you take on those new skills, new steps, new places, and new faces, which are custom designed for the advancement and acceleration of your purpose, passion, and, designed dream life, your scent of the rain and essence of hope will grow stronger and stronger each day.

Step 4: Move On. Be the Change You Want to See in the World—With Passion

Naomi moved on. She moved on first geographically, and subsequently, she transitioned internally to not sabotage her new adventure. William Bridges, a great author on change, has noted that it isn't the changes that do one in, it's the transitions. Change is not the same as transition. Change is situational. Change is a new job, a new home, a new car, a new spouse, a new state to live in. However, the transition is internal. It took God only a day or so to take the Israelites out of Egypt, but it took more than 40 years for God to get Egypt out of Israel. In other words, if your mind is not "out," then you're not "out," regardless of where you are...there you are.

Naomi moved on, and so must we. Naomi moved on with a persevering passion for surviving and later to thrive within the homeland of her return. Her vision of her life had been cut to the very stump. However, she smelled the scent of rain and began to dream again—bigger. Her instructions unto her daughter-in-law, Ruth, as to how to propose unto Boaz the rich landowner whose fields she had worked in, reveal unto us that the bud of purpose, passion, and life has grown bigger. She had learned to hold a vision for her life lightly because a vision can always be changed, enhanced, and reformed.

If we are too attached to one particular vision, then we close our minds to the possibility that there may be more out there—an even better vision within our reach. If we convince ourselves that a single, predetermined vision is the only option, then we are, in essence wearing blinders. And it's effortless to do. Focused vision points us in the right direction, as Naomi returned to her hometown of Bethlehem. They tell us which way to go and how to get there. Holding our visions loosely enough keeps us open to the immense opportunity that surrounds us. Upon hearing that Ruth has been gleaning from the fields of Boaz and had found favor in his eyes, Naomi's revived purpose and passion gave her the capacity for enlarged creativity to think of a brilliant idea once acted upon resulted in a brand new chapter of revised purpose, passion, and life for her. She became a grandmother!

Naomi's renewed passion came not only from the outside but as well as from within. Passion is what gives us the desire to turn visions into reality. "And Naomi took the child, and laid it in her bosom, and became nurse unto it. And the women her neighbors gave it a name saying 'There is a son born unto Naomi, and they called his name Obed; he is the father of Jesse, the father of David'" (Ruth 4:16-17). Who would have ever thought that Naomi would become the great-grandmother of the greatest king of Israel—David? How is Naomi's bitterness healed? In such a way that she let go of the destructive self-identity of being called "Mara" or "bitter."

She is once again, Naomi: no longer seeing her life as one that is bitter. She now sees and experiences the "sweet life." How? The answer is in Verses 16-17. In offering the infant boy the sweetness of her breast, her own life is revived and sweetened at the hand of God—Shaddai (see Genesis 49:25), the breasty one who satisfies and replenishes her breast with milk as well as her life with renewed nourishment, significance, and purpose. It is in the giving of oneself to others that we truly are living. One can give without loving, but one can't love without giving.

There is yet hope for a tree if it is cut. At the scent of rain, it will bud again.

Hold on. Let go. Take on and move on.

My friend, there is yet hope for you today. I am ever confident that as you actualize these four steps into your life, you will surely smell the scent of rain, the essence of hope, and your purpose, passion, and life will bud again!

By Matthew West

There is no guilt here.
There is no shame.
No pointing fingers.
There is no blame.
What happened yesterday has disappeared.

The dirt has washed away, and now it's clear.
There's only grace.
There's only love.
There's only mercy, and believe me, it's enough.
Your sins are gone without a trace
There's nothing left now.
There's only grace.

You're starting over now under the sun.
You're stepping forward now.
A new life has begun;
Your new life has begun

And if you should fall again
Get back up, get back up.
Reach out and take my hand.

Get back up, get back up.

NOTES

Chapter 2:
1. Journal of American Medical Association

Chapter 4:
1. Bear,I.J:R.G.Thomas (March 1964) "Nature of Argillaceous odor." 201(4923):993-995
2. Bear,I.J:R.G.Thomas (March 1964) "Nature of Argillaceous odor." 201(4923):993-995

Chapter 5:
1. J.Gerald Janzen "At the Scent of Water, The Ground of Hope in the book of Job." 101-103
2. J.Gerald Janzen "At the Scent of Water, The Ground of Hope in the book of Job." 110
3. J.Gerald Janzen "At the Scent of Water, The Ground of Hope in the book of Job" 125

Chapter 6:
1. Max Lucado "Bold Love." Chapter 2.

Chapter 8:
1. Richard Rohr excerpts "In Hope against Darkness)

ACKNOWLEDGMENTS

For the past ten years, since I started writing this book, the following people have been most instrumental in being the scent of rain and essence of hope unto my "dead stump" that had been cut, wounded, and deeply scarred. Without them and their invaluable individual nourishment unto my soul, this plant would most likely have never "bud again."

To my wife, Marianne: From the moment I first met you, walking down the paved pathway to the fellowship hall of the Zion Bible Institute, wearing your European hat, I smelled the scent of rain for love. You were the most beautiful girl I had ever seen. You were the scent of rain unto me. You gave me hope that love would "bud again."

This book could have never been written without you, and for that, I am most thankful.

I know I don't say it nearly often enough, but you've been God's primary instrument to shape and mold my life to what it is today. If there are any for whom my words, written or spoken, bring the "scent of rain" unto—it is most largely because of you. You've challenged me to love better, live bigger, and lead more brilliantly.

When I think of our three most fantastic, brilliant, and beautiful children: **Joshua**, **Hannah**, and **Sarah**, I'm most grateful for your outstanding outpouring of faith, hope, and love into their lives. Your life of prayer and pursuit of godliness, I'm confident, will result in an ever-increasing inheritance of godly, brilliant, history-makers who make a world of difference in this life and the life to come. Thank you.

To my Dad and Mom, Ken and Deanna Simons: Their unwavering support, unconditional love, and constant prayers have been the "life support" and east wind which ushered in the "scent of rain" back into my life so I would bud again.

It has been said that a real friend is one who walks in when the rest of the world walked out. I can never forget my Dad telling me that one of life's greatest riches that I would discover was not in the bank account, the size of one's house, or the wheels on a car but the number of "real friends" one would have. He said if I had two or three, I'd be a wealthy man. It took me 40 years to discover the truth in that. I consider myself "rich."

And so I'm so very thankful for my real friends. Friendship isn't about whom you've known the longest. It's about who walked into your life and said, "I'm here for you" and proved it.

Bob Westenberg: You walked into my life at such a critical junction in time at the Hudson Institute of Santa Barbara. You listened to me and nourished my soul unto new buds of life with your friendship. You encouraged me to develop my understanding of "the scent of rain" resulting in the creation of the Petrichor Partners Infinitely Better Living Seminar and Petrichor Partners.

Dr. Joseph Umidi: You walked into my life at the time of most challenge & opportunity and remained a most nourishing nutrient of hope and encouragement. Your mentorship, partnership, and friendship in my life brought the "scent of rain and essence of hope " to my deeply cut heart and soul. Thank you for including the Infinitely Better Living Seminar on the shelf of your world-class coaching resources.

Stephen Potutschnig: Your most genuine pure friendship since 1985 has been a true testament that geographical distance does not determine the quality of friendship. Friendship is a matter of the heart, not a matter of miles. While you served as a missionary in Bolivia and a pastor in the U.S.A., the roots of our friendship have lengthened and grown in spite of the countries and states which have been between us. Thank you.

Erik Tammaru: Your constant friendship has spanned two continents and 25 years, both as a missionary and as a pastor. Your invitation and permission for me to serve you strategically while you pastored your church have been the scent of rain. For that, I am most grateful.

Richard Sfameni: Your friendship and partnership throughout the past 30 years have been most nourishing. Your strategic, most timely gift to me in my last ministry trip to your church has been most invaluable. Thank you for giving me the book *Rebuilding your Broken World* by Gordon MacDonald. It has been said that a book is a great book because it introduces itself to you at the time you need it the most. I can only hope that this book *The Scent of Rain—Essence of Hope* might be a "great book" for someone else as the book you gave unto me.

Danny Thomas: What can I say? Thank you for being a gift that keeps on giving. Your life and life message "Rumble, rumble, I'm a tank" profoundly and permanently influenced my life. Your gift of open friendship, your invitation two years ago to visit and minister with you for several days was life-giving. One of the most beautiful qualities of true friendship is to understand and be understood. You "get me."

Loren Dunfee: Life is better when you're laughing. You've given me the gift of laughter ever since we were roommates in Zion Bible Institute. Thank you for being my friend. Thank you for making me laugh.

Karen Shorey, my sister: A sister is a gift to the heart and a friend to the spirit. Thank you for your enduring friendship that is ever-growing and deepening. You've become an amazing woman, one whom I'm so proud to call "my sister."

ABOUT THE AUTHOR

E. David Simons is a diverse professional. Missionary, pastor, life coach, sales consultant, and author. Communicating hope: creating life transformational environments and experiences spanning sixteen countries and five continents have been his footprint. He is known as "the Encourager." He presently resides in the greater St. Louis area with his wife Marianne and three children Joshua, Hannah, and Sarah. Visit www.petrichorpartners.com or connect to him on Facebook at Edavid Simons.

www.ingramcontent.com/pod-product-compliance
Lightning Source LLC
LaVergne TN
LVHW091201080426
835509LV00006B/769